A Spiritual Look at the 12 Signs

An Introduction to Spiritual Astrology

A Spiritual Look
at the 12 Signs

An Introduction to Spiritual Astrology

Joseph Polansky

Winchester, UK
Washington, USA

First published by Dodona Books, 2017
Dodona Books is an imprint of John Hunt Publishing Ltd., Laurel House, Station Approach,
Alresford, Hants, SO24 9JH, UK
office1@jhpbooks.net
www.johnhuntpublishing.com
www.dodona-books.com

For distributor details and how to order please visit the 'Ordering' section on our website.

ISBN: 978 1 78099 199 3
978 1 78099 200 6 (ebook)
Library of Congress Control Number: 2016949860

A CIP catalogue record for this book is available from the British Library.

Design: Stuart Davies

Printed and bound by CPI Group (UK) Ltd, Croydon, CR0 4YY, UK

We operate a distinctive and ethical publishing philosophy in all
areas of our business, from our global network of authors to
production and worldwide distribution.

CONTENTS

Also by Joseph Polansky

Pendulum Power (with Greg Nielsen)
The Moving Universe
Sun Sign Success
Your Personal Horoscope Series
The Magic Stone
The Graduate
A Technique for Meditation
Daily Star Planner
Healing Meditation Audio CD

Lovingly dedicated to the Twelve Lords of the Life Power

Introduction

Astrology is essentially a spiritual science. But because of the way it has been presented – especially here in the West – the Western reader has lost sight of this. Hopefully this work will help to correct the misperception.

This is not your typical Sun sign book. Having authored many Sun sign books, I know the difference. In the typical Sun sign book, the signs are described in terms of behavioral characteristics – i.e. Aries are impetuous and rash, Capricorns are controlling and ambitious, Pisces are dreamy, Geminis talkative etc., etc., etc. Often they are judgmental – depending on the mindset of the author. Though these descriptions are valid, so far as they go, the spiritual root causes for these behaviors are left out. Why is Pisces so dreamy and otherworldly? Why are Geminis so talkative? Why are Aries rash and impetuous? It all seems so arbitrary. Little wonder that Astrology is in disrepute in many quarters. The logic behind these things is never explained.

It is only when we understand Astrology as a spiritual science that everything becomes clear. All the behaviors and characteristics of the different signs are eminently rational. For there is a spiritual purpose behind them. These behaviors are the Divine itself seeking to express itself along certain lines and to achieve certain ends. Even the so-called pathologies of the different signs are not pathologies as we understand it. Generally they are Divine gifts and urges – very positive things – that are either overused or misused. Often, they are gifts misunderstood by others and the label "pathology" is placed on it. The Divine is working through a mortal personality and it is the mortal mind that distorts the benevolent flow of the Divine impulse. But the original urge – the impulse – is holy and divine.

The Great Creator created the universe in a certain way, with certain laws. These laws – and the laws of Astrology are part and

1

parcel of them – do not deny the creator as so many try to claim. They no more deny the creator than the laws of physics or mathematics do. Anything that is part of the original creation cannot be the "work of the devil." However, if the knowledge is misused or abused – as has often been the case throughout history – then yes, it can certainly be turned to diabolical uses. But of itself Astrology is pristine and pure and has always fascinated the greatest minds of every generation.

Because of the spiritual nature of Astrology, some have made a religion out of it. This too seems to me to be error. The Wisdom of the stars stands above all religion. Yet, it does not deny any of them. It is the fount from which all religions proceed. In certain ages one way to worship is emphasized. In other ages, different nuances of worship, different aspects of the Divine, are emphasized. Every religious path can be seen in the Horoscope. Further, a given person's attraction to a certain path can also be seen. See the chapter "The Twelve Yogas" for more detail.

One of the problems with Sun sign books is that rarely do we find anyone who is "purely" one sign or another. Generally we are a mix of different signs. The Sun can be in Aries, but the native will have many planets in Taurus or Pisces. In such cases the person will behave more like a Taurus or Pisces than an Aries. If you know your Horoscope you can read the signs that apply to you. If you don't, it might be advisable to have your personal horoscope done. This will add more accuracy to the interpretations.

If the reader comes away from this book with a deeper understanding of who he or she is, a deeper understanding of what Astrology is all about, if the self-condemnation and judgment are removed, then my job has been done.

Joseph Polansky

A Spiritual View of Aries

The central urge of Aries is to begin new things. The soul, symbolically speaking, has just completed a major cycle. It has digested its past. It has "died to the old." In Aries the soul is "reborn" or "resurrected" into a new cycle of life, growth and experience.

If we meditate on the sunrise or Spring or on newly born infants we can get a feeling of what the Aries nature is all about.

Aries is the spirit of "youth unconquerable." There is something of the spirit of eternal youth about them. Though they grow and mature they never quite grow up. In the rare cases where they do grow "old" it is never "gracefully." Aries is fighting that state furiously. It is not their nature. Not in their psychology. "Everything in nature – including old age and hoary tradition – can be overcome by my will," sayeth Aries. This is as it should be. For Aries is here to learn about itself and its power through experience – through doing – through action.

Many astrologers say that Aries is a soul with no "past at its back" – and this is very true. As far as it is concerned all the "lessons of history" – the imposing weight of past tradition – do not exist. And if the Aries acknowledges its existence he/she feels it's "irrelevant." To talk to Aries about the lessons of history is like trying to convince the sunrise about the tradition of night; or trying to delay the Spring with talk about the great tradition of Winter. "All of this may be true," says Aries, "but MY coming shall change all that!"

Aries is the soul eternally on the rise – always on the rise – never at its peak – though it is destined for the peaks. But in order for it to reach the peaks that it KNOWS MUST happen, the Aries will have to undergo many a metamorphosis – many learning experiences.

In Aries, symbolically speaking, the soul "remembers" its "I

AM THAT I AMNESS" – its divine individuality. Unconditioned and unconditional being. "I can do and be whatever I will and no man has the right to stop me from expressing the Law of my Being." I am who I am and the world had better accept me as I am or there's going to be a fight. Perhaps no one more than Aries understands the ageless dictum of being "true to oneself." Perhaps no one more than Aries lives this truth in experience.

This is perhaps why Aries natives are generally unsuited and unhappy in corporate environments. For if there is one inviolate rule in the corporate boardroom it is this – "Thou shalt never be thyself. Thou shalt conform to the image and likeness that we create for thee." (We are talking about the Aries type. This can be modified by the individual horoscope.)

There are those who call Aries "rash and impulsive," but it seems to me that this is an unfair judgment. True that from the viewpoint of more staid types Aries' behavior is rash, impatient and impulsive, but the Aries native does not consider him/herself this way. Aries is just being itself. Speed – what others call speed – is normal. The only way to be. Where do we draw the line between "speed-alacrity-alertness" and rashness-impulsiveness? Who is to make that judgment?

Is the Sun rash when it banishes the night? Is Spring rash when it banishes Winter?

From the psychological viewpoint, the Aries nature tends to define itself in terms of "what it can do." There are no limits to what I am if I can do it. To try to limit or curtail the activities of Aries – which are really explorations of itself – is to limit the "I AMNESS" of Aries. And they generally resent it bitterly. The joy of the action is its own reason for doing it. Never mind whether the action has "redeeming social value" – never mind whether the action is really needed or not – never mind whether the action is profitable or not (though the Aries sincerely hopes that it will be) – action is good for its own sake. If my action produces some "social benefit" or profit for the shareholders all the better – a happy side effect – but the bliss is in the doing. Profit or social benefit is not really the main objective. The joy of the doing is. Very often the Aries will use the pretext of some social good as a cover for its need for action. They are the activists par excellence of the zodiac.

In the more evolved types they are karma yogis. They express the Divine through action – through deeds. This is a valid spiritual path for Aries.

The path of contemplation, silence and stillness is not for them and thus most Aries types have some trouble with most meditative paths. They need to meditate while doing something. They learn by doing.

Aries rules the head. For in the head, all experience, all cycles, and all manifestations find their beginnings. Everything begins in the head. And just as thoughts spring forth spontaneously in the head (thought is the "activity" of the head) effortlessly and naturally, so, too, do actions spring forth from Aries spontaneously and naturally.

The color of Aries is red, the first color of the spectrum, the hottest and most active of all the colors. The gems of Aries are amethyst, rubies and garnets. Its metals are iron and steel.

The most favorable periods of the year for Aries are March 21 – April 21 (Sun in Aries); July 21 – August 21 (Sun in Leo); November 21 – December 21 (Sun in Sagittarius).[1] The most favorable periods of the month are when the Moon is in Aries, Leo or Sagittarius. The best days of the week for Aries are Tuesday and Sunday. (Again, this will be modified by other indicators in the horoscope. But a Tuesday with good aspects will be better for Aries than a Wednesday or Friday with good aspects. A period when the Sun is in Leo (July 21 – August 21), for example, with good aspects, will be better for Aries than other periods with equivalent aspects.)

Speaking generally, for this can be modified by many other factors in the horoscope, Aries' genius is in execution, not planning. If there is a clear-cut plan presented to them they can execute it perfectly, but if you ask them to "create a plan" there could be problems. It's not that they can't plan – to them, with their genius of action, these things seem "unnecessary, irrelevant, too abstract, too time-wasting, too procrastinating." They are "field men" par excellence, but not very good "staff men."

If you want to punish an Aries – we hope it never comes to that – make him/her a vice-president and stick him/her behind a desk all day.

The willfulness and so-called self-centeredness of Aries is never malicious. It is the willfulness (some have called it omnipotence) of the infant who KNOWS – by its instincts – EXACTLY what its job is for the stage that it's in. The infant is so "in tune" with the Divine Will – so "true to itself" – that all around it, even powerful adults, must conform to its dictates. It is the willfulness of the dawn banishing the night. So it is with Aries. They know that they are here to do things and to learn by doing.

Even if they make mistakes, they will only know that it is a mistake through the doing. No good to tell them about it beforehand. They have to find out about it for themselves. After they've done the thing, then they might agree that "yes, possibly it was a mistake." But don't YOU start telling them beforehand. The Aries will see it as a "limitation of his/her will" and will either do it anyway – or if forced to obey, will chafe under the inaction.

The herbs of Aries are aloe, garlic, onions, cayenne pepper, jalapenos, radishes and mustard. Its scent is honeysuckle.

Reflexology points important to Aries are the thumbs of both hands (from the nails to the top joint) and the big toes of both feet. These should be massaged regularly – but especially during stressful transits. Regular face and scalp massage (also cranial sacral therapy) is excellent for Aries.

Careers most suitable for Aries are welding, metal working, sheep herding, the wool industry, surgeons, the military, athletics, any pioneering enterprise – the riskier the better, the hat industry, barber or beautician (if Venus is strong in the nativity). In the corporate world they are better as field executives than staff executives. They will naturally gravitate to jobs that offer "risk and adventure." They will excel at positions where "initiative and quick reflexes" are the most important consideration.

The Aries nature is very self-motivated and very often they are able to motivate others – to fire them up with zeal and enthusiasm – to banish fear and depression in others. Difficult to be in the "doldrums" with an Aries around.

Meditation for Aries

"I Am that I Am hath sent me into this world. I Am that I Am hath sent ME into expression. Therefore, my actions are ever potent, ever successful, ever victorious, ever benevolent, and ever harmonious. I Am that I Am forever acts through me. I Am that I Am is the real doer, the real achiever in me."

A Spiritual View of Taurus

In its journey through the zodiac the soul, symbolically speaking, is discovering new powers – new things about itself – gaining experience.

In Aries the soul discovers or "remembers" its power to ACT, and like any newly discovered "toy" the tendency is to want to play with it – to explore it – to its ultimate capacity. The result of the action – in terms of profits, or social benefits, or "good" achieved – is not the issue with Aries. The joy of the action – the joy of the doing – is where it's at.

In Taurus the soul still has the power to act but something new is discovered or recalled. It has the power to ESTABLISH and SOLIDIFY an action or group of actions on the Earth. It has the power to do and it also has the power not to do.

When in doubt an Aries will "do something" – almost a "knee jerk" reaction. When in doubt a Taurus will tend "to do nothing." It has learned its lessons in Aries – doing something is not always the answer – sometimes it is, sometimes it isn't. Having learned from its over-exuberance in Aries, the Taurus wants to be absolutely sure of things before launching any action on the physical plane – especially actions that could affect its security and comfort – something that is very vital and important to Taurus.

If we observe the behavior of any "reformed" person – a reformed alcoholic, or reformed drug addict or reformed smoker – we note a tendency to actually abhor their former state. These people tend to be the most rabid anti-smokers or anti-alcohol people. The reformed "sinner" tends to be the most fanatic churchman. In order to break from a former state the soul needs to embrace its "polar opposite" and sometimes it becomes extreme in another direction before equilibrium is established. The Taurus nature could, in a certain sense, be considered a "reformed action addict." He/she seems to actually abhor action – to abhor anything that smacks of pioneering. The tendency can be to an ultra-conservatism which is just as unbalanced as too much activism. "One should not lightly trifle with a comfort that is already manifest," sayeth Taurus. "Holy, holy, holy is the status quo."

But Taurus has this outstanding virtue. It remembers the essential wealth and affluence of the soul. It remembers – instinctively – that there is no lack, poverty or want in the spiritual dimensions of being; that the laws of the cosmos operating through nature are always working to enrich and prosper; and that every soul has access to sure and steady SUPPORT. The Taurus nature knows of its inner wealth and recognizes its inalienable right to it. It recognizes the eternal ease and comfort of its higher nature and that two of the qualities of Divinity (which we are all here to express in one way or another) are wealth and affluence. Having. Owning. "The Earth is the Lord's and the fullness thereof, and I being ONE with the Lord of ALL partake and share in this universal ownership. I am a natural shareholder in Earth Incorporated." Thus does the Taurus think to himself.

And the Taurus' instinct is to express this spiritual state and perception on the Earth. This, in my opinion, is the key to Taurus.

In the younger soul this gets a bit distorted. The Taurus can tend to define itself in terms of what it has. I am what I own. I am my bank balance. I am what my financial statement shows. I own therefore I am. If the stock market goes down then I have "become less than I am" – I am diminished by it.

The more developed Taurus thinks differently. I am therefore I own. I own everything that my Father in heaven owns. I own because my soul is eternally affluent – such is its inherent nature. There is no pride or ego in this ownership; it just IS that way. Being is impossible without having the substance to be, and if I

AM then the substance of Being is also present. Possessions are a natural attribute of my being. Matter is very spiritual! Wealth is spiritual! There is no evil in it or about it!

No matter what happens on the physical plane, the instant I make my connection with "my Father who owns it all" I am again part owner – an honored and important shareholder – in all the wealth there is.

We are all very grateful to our Taureans for reminding us of this and expressing this truth in their lives. In Taurus the virtues of the element Earth are especially pronounced. Prudence, carefulness, the power to "materialize" ideas, the love and respect for form, conservatism, solidity and stability are all attributed to Taurus. For Taurus is the fertile, fecund, productive Earth. Earth as the substance of spirit. Earth as the "scene of events" through which mighty spiritual powers act.

The developed Taurus will smile indulgently at some of us "star gazers." It is a non-malicious, tolerant smile. It is a smile of one who knows a great secret and is ready to reveal it to us as soon as we are ready to hear.

"Why are you gazing at the stars, young man? Don't you know that all their wonderful secrets and laws and riches are right here under your feet? Don't you know that the ground you stand on is holy ground? When will you take off your shoes? You are already in the Promised Land. Don't you know that the Earth which you have for so long despised is the ultimate objective of Spirit? That Spirit not only loves the Earth, but longs to materialize and concretize? That Spirit wants to be Earthed?

"Come with me. In my garden are all the secrets of the cosmos. In man's financial activities are all the laws of nature. In the visible we see the invisible. Do you think that you can escape Earth? The principle of Earth exists in the Highest Heavens, just as the entire cosmos exists in the Earth. Earth is the temple of the Most High. Look at me properly and I shall grow wings.

"Every tree is a fire of God. Every rock the incarnation of an avatar. Every movement the activity of One Mover. Every mineral the body of a planetary spirit. If you cannot find Truth here, where will you find it? If you cannot find the kingdom of heaven here you will not find it anywhere."

Thus speaks the illuminated Taurus. He has much to teach us.

Taurus excels in careers where stability, routine, persistence, and tireless stick-to-it-iveness are essential. They are excellent executives and managers, better as staff executives than out in the field. They excel in farming, agriculture, and real estate. The cattle industry, banking, sculpture, carpentry, architecture, massage and singing are also excellent professions. They are fabulous money managers. If other factors in the horoscope are right they can excel in the arts.

The gems of Taurus are emeralds and coral. Its metal is copper. Its scents are rose and vanilla. Its herbs are red roses, vanilla, coltsfoot, columbine, lilies, and daisies.

Taurus rules the throat – the place where the body takes possession of the elements of nature – in the form of food – that belong to it. The throat is the place where physical substance enters the body. It is also the place (vocal cords) where abstract or invisible thoughts concretize and materialize as words and sounds – fixed forms of thought. If we meditate on the throat region we will not only understand Taurus, but we will also understand what wealth is about and how it is produced – word by word.

The reflexology points for Taurus are the base of both thumbs and the base of both big toes. These should be squeezed and massaged regularly – but especially when there are stressful aspects to the native's power points in Taurus or to Venus. In the center of the shoulders are points that also reflex to the throat. Regular neck massage – and cranial sacral therapy – is powerful for Taurus.

The most favorable periods in the year are April 21 – May 21 (Sun in Taurus); August 22 – September 21 (Sun in Virgo);

December 21 – January 21 (Sun in Capricorn). The most favorable times of the month are when the Moon is in Taurus, Virgo or Capricorn. The best day of the week for Taurus is Friday. Monday is also pretty good. The most favorable hours of a day are the hours of Venus and when Taurus, Virgo or Capricorn is rising. (It is understood that this is modified by the individual horoscope and by the daily transits. But a Friday with good aspects will be better than other days with good aspects and if there is choice in the matter we would choose Friday or Monday for an important activity. The same is true when considering the periods of the year. Sun in Taurus, Virgo or Capricorn are better than Sun in most other signs given an "equivalence" of aspects. If the native is in a generally "easy" period, it will tend to be even easier when the Sun or Moon is in Taurus, Virgo or Capricorn.)

Meditation for Taurus

"The Earth is the Lord's and the fullness thereof. The cattle on a thousand hills are mine. All that the Father – the God within – has, I have. I am a co-owner and co-administrator of all the riches of heaven and earth. Wealth is a law of my being. It is one of the natural attributes of my soul. I am wealthy because the mind of God is wealthy and I am a point through which it expresses its harmonious and lawful wealth here on Earth. This is the source of my wealth and well-being. This wealth does not rust, rot or diminish, nor can thieves steal or corrupt it. I am wealthy on the outside because I am wealthy on the inside. I am wealthy financially and in friendships. I am wealthy materially and mentally. I own all Divine Ideas. And in this realm I can own ALL and ALL would still be left for others. Therefore I am fearless and secure and there is no greed in my consciousness. I am happy wealth. I am harmonious wealth. I am at ease in my wealth. And though someday I will have to let go of the outer symbols of my wealth, the spiritual equivalents that come from within shall be ever with me."

A Spiritual View of Gemini

In Gemini the soul becomes conscious of another of its many powers – its power to think and to communicate its thought in language so that other minds can understand it. It is a formidable power which is easily abused.

This is the power that links different minds together, not only in space but in time. This is the power that makes TRADE possible between humans. This is the power – in its rudimentary form – that makes all civilization and progress possible. No wonder the Gemini is totally fascinated by it!

We have to understand each sign in terms of where it came from and where it is heading. Gemini has to be understood as a direct progression of Taurus – an elaboration of the Taurus experience. A widening of the power discovered in Taurus.

The Gemini, symbolically speaking, has undergone the experiences of Aries and Taurus. It has experienced the joys of action. It has experienced the wealth of Taurus and knows of its power to create wealth. But the relatively isolated wealth of Taurus is not enough for Gemini. In order to really be wealthy one must be able to trade one's surpluses to others in return for their surpluses. By oneself one cannot eat all the wealth of Taurus. It would just go to waste. However, if I can trade my excess to others in exchange for things that would further enrich my life, my wealth and quality of life are truly increased. In order to do this, language is necessary. We must be able to communicate to other minds in other marketplaces in order to make these trades. And so the beginning of intellectual development takes place.

In Gemini the soul perhaps does not yet realize the ramifications of such a step – the development of mind. It sees such development, at this stage, as purely in its own self-interest. Language is most definitely a profitable proposition. Very practical and useful. Those with verbal facility and intellectual gifts rise to the top in any society. Facility with languages gives one access to other minds – and most importantly to other IDEAS.

In Gemini the soul has found a new toy – a fascinating and powerful toy – and is completely engrossed with it. Very understandable. The Gemini with its words and ideas is like the adolescent who has just discovered sex. It dominates the mind. It is SO WONDERFUL. What are its limits? How far can I go with it? I don't want to do anything else except explore this. NOTHING is more interesting than this.

So, this exploration of the intellect – really, only the portal to real mental development – leads to all kinds of accidents, mishaps, and abuses – also to some genuine learning. The Gemini discovers that one can manipulate others with words; that words can be used to express truth or to express falsity; one can use words to trick others and to achieve any advantage one chooses over another. One can wage war with words and do more damage perhaps than with mere physical abuse. The pen is indeed mightier than the sword. One can use words to inform or to "disinform." Images and attitudes are created with words – images and attitudes that can affect not only the exchange of goods and services but the destiny of whole nations as well. Words aptly used create public opinion before which even the mightiest conqueror bows.

Reality itself can be changed or even created by the Law of the Word. The Gemini, perhaps more than any other sign, understands the magic of words. The temptations for Gemini are very great – for in this realm he/she is a real power. He/she has a definite advantage over other types. How will Gemini use this advantage?

Once intellectual or mental development is begun there is nothing for mankind to do but to continue with it and develop it to its ultimate level – and this is really infinite. In vain do many mystics, bhaktis, "love, love, love types" rail against the intellect, try all kinds of means to subvert it – short circuit it – circumvent it. This is a legitimate and important power of the soul. A divine power if you will.

Like any other power it is neither good nor evil. It is strictly a question of how it is used. Used correctly, it is the mechanism by which all progress is made. As Korzybski rightly observes, it is the way humans "bind time" – the way civilization transcends the time dimension.[2] Because of language – written and spoken – every generation of humans can begin where the old generation left off. The new generation has access – by means of books, tapes, records, magazines, etc. – to all the knowledge of the previous one. Thus it is not necessary to "re-invent the wheel" in every generation. We can go on to new things. Today every school child knows more about physics than Isaac Newton, more about geometry than Euclid, more about computers than George Boole. This is not to take anything away from these great men, but the modern school child has access not only to everything that these men knew but also to all the later developments in the fields – to developments that came after them. Our grandchildren will know more physics than Einstein by the same principle.

It is an awesome power that our Gemini types play with so glibly and innocently.

The symbol for Gemini is the twins. This expresses the duality or dual nature of the mental processes. The intellect functions only by "duality" – by ratios, by comparison of one thing to another. Without "duality" intellectual thought could not take place. Those who are skilled in the dialectic understand this clearly. Every mental position – every proposition – every assertion – has, on the intellectual level, its polar opposite. The intellect is indeed two-faced – not because of its essential "evil or malice" but because this is its nature. Those who have scaled the heights of intellectual achievement know that every duality "gives birth" to a new "synthesis" that unites the opposite polarities. The new synthesis embraces BOTH sides and makes them a part of a "larger unity." The two opposites become ONE. And this is the path that Gemini must take to unify the two sides of its nature.

So the Gemini can indeed seem to be "two-faced" not only to his/her friends but also to him/herself. But if he/she realizes that this is not "schizophrenia" (though it can lead to this if no attempt at union is made) but two aspects of something "higher," an integration of the character will take place.

It takes a while for Gemini to understand that its rational and linguistic powers need to be handled as delicately and consciously as one would handle any other power – whether it be a gun, or car or airplane, etc. But eventually they do.

Descartes, brilliant though he was, expresses the attitude of the younger Gemini soul – "I think therefore I Am." There is identification with the thought processes as being "ME." But the more mature Gemini holds the opposite – "I Am, therefore I think." It seems like a fine distinction, but in reality there is a world of difference. In Descartes' case being arises from thought – thought is the primary, being the result. The truth is that being comes before thought. If there is no being there can be no thought. First I Am (Aries) then I Think (Gemini). Being is more than thought, though thought is one of the primary powers of being.

The Gemini is the media person par excellence. They make excellent teachers, writers, interpreters, speech therapists, journalists, salesmen, advertising executives, and public relations people. Any industry concerned with education and/or communications – word processors, typewriters, computers – hardware or software, facsimile machines, telephones, telegraphs, telexes, radio, TV, printing is good for them.

The best periods of the year for Gemini are May 21 – June 21 (Sun in Gemini); September 21 – October 22 (Sun in Libra);

January 21 – February 20 (Sun in Aquarius). Best days of the month are when the Moon is in Gemini, Libra or Aquarius. Best day of the week is Wednesday. The most favorable hours of the day are the hours of Mercury and when Gemini, Libra or Aquarius are rising. (It is understood that the individual horoscope and transits will definitely modify what we say here. But these periods, if there are good aspects, will be better than other periods with equally good aspects.)

Gemini's gem is aquamarine. Its metal is quicksilver. Its herbs are carrots, celery, caraway, fennel, madder, meadowsweet, tansy, vervain, woodbine and yarrow.

Reflexology points important to Gemini are the pads of the palms (both hands) directly beneath the base of the middle and fourth fingers. On the feet, the balls of the foot directly beneath the middle and fourth toes. These are the reflexes to the lungs and bronchial tubes, ruled by Mercury. These should be massaged regularly. The arms and shoulders should also be massaged regularly and especially when there is unusual planetary stress.

Meditation for Gemini

"My words are Spirit and they are Truth and they do not return unto me void, but accomplish whereunto they are sent. I know that my words are words of power. They created my reality up to this point in my life and are capable of creating new, better and more pleasing realities. I am careful of this great power and use it wisely to bless and to benefit myself and those around me. My words have the power of conjuring images in my mind and in the minds of others. My words, through my subconscious mind, activate mighty cosmic forces, which bring to me in the form of events, things and experiences, exactly what I have spoken – and the intention I had when speaking them. Therefore I am careful to say what I mean and to mean what I say. The same Mind that spoke the universe into existence speaks its words through me and thinks its thoughts through me. I am receptive to that Mind now and allow it to guide me to greater understanding of the power of my word. I now speak only those words that I would like to see happen in my experience."

A Spiritual View of Cancer

The soul has about talked itself out in Gemini. It has danced on the glittering superficies of the intellectual peaks. It has mastered the mental acrobatics of Gemini and is ready for something new – the experience of Cancer. The discovery of the dimension of feeling. And what a dimension it is!

If the Gemini has been honest with himself he has discovered that logic and thought – powerful though they are – are not everything. If he/she has been honestly introspective he has discovered the power of mood – feeling – emotional states; and he has discovered their subtle, but powerful impact on his thought.

In certain moods he cannot think as clearly as in other moods. In certain states of mind his vaunted logic is inexplicably "overruled" – out-powered! When logic dictates that he follow a certain course he finds – inexplicably – that he tends NOT to behave as his logic dictates. Something is definitely amiss here!

Moreover, he finds that brilliant though his logic is, very often he does not "FEEL" as he thinks. More and more he discovers that he talks one way while feeling quite a different way. Another dimension has brought itself to his/her awareness. What's wrong here? Nothing. The soul is entering the experience of Cancer – the dimension of feeling the psychological dimension.

Though Canceriens don't often display it, they are very capable of the intellectual brilliance of Gemini – for Cancer is a further progression of Gemini. But the Cancerien feels that "I've graduated from that – I've had enough verbal masturbation. I want to explore the deep things – I want to explore why I feel the way I feel – I want to understand my moods – I want to feel rather than think – if my thinking goes along with my feeling, all well and good, but if there is conflict I'm going to go with my gut feeling. I don't want to think about life – I want to feel life!"

"Feelings are more real and more powerful than thoughts," says Cancer.

"My feelings are REALITY to me."

"My feeling of me IS me!" says Cancer. "If I FEEL well, I AM well!"

Indeed there is a great element of truth here. But the Cancerien – needing to develop and explore this new power dimension – tends to err too much on the side of feeling. Just as Gemini errs too much on the side of thought, and Aries on the side of activity. But this is understandable. For this dimension and faculty is like a new toy – and new toys are there to be explored, to be played with, to learn with, to make mistakes with.

To the sign of Cancer, astrologers attribute the maternal instinct – the instinct – the need – the urge and the power to nurture and protect those that are weaker than ourselves. Here we find the urge and need to create families and tribes and clans. Here the soul discovers that "wealth of feeling" is also wealth.

So the Cancer type has a great need for family and family life. Its emotional well-being depends on the support it gets from its family, tribe and clan. Every Cancerien has a deep need to have their own family. If they cannot have one physically they will join or create a "spiritual family" or a "corporate family."

The family is one of nature's survival mechanisms. It is the way that nature bonds disparate entities by some common bond – either of blood or of tribe or of race, religion or nation. This kind of grouping is very natural and this is one of the functions of the Cancer type.

They bring this thinking even into their economic lives. They thrive in corporate environments that are run like a family. They love a "family business."

If we inquire as to what it is that is essential in the creation of families we will find that it is a strong common "feeling" about things. The feeling can be one of blood, but it can also be a strong feeling about God, or nation, or about art or philosophy. People who share the same feelings about things are part of a family on the inner planes of existence.

Every family has dominant members and relatively weaker members. If the stronger devoured the weaker – or exploited the weaker without regard to their best interests – the family would soon not exist. This is especially so in the case of members who are young and growing and who cannot defend themselves – i.e. children. And so, the maternal instinct – which has very deep roots in life logic – prevents that sort of thing. In fact it tends to go overboard in the opposite direction.

"Do what you want to do," says Cancer, "but do not hurt my home, children or family!"

Without "emotional sensitivity" it is doubtful whether any home or family could exist.

The sign of Cancer also has important things to teach us metaphysically – about the way reality is created. In the demonstration of the Laws of Mind we start off with a sense of "I Am" (Aries) which recognizes that it already possesses the "Mental Substance" necessary for creation (Taurus) which leads to a "Speaking of the Word" – a thought (Gemini) which leads to the "Feeling" of the finished thing (Cancer) which leads to the birth of the new "Child" or manifestation (Leo).

"There's a logic behind every strong feeling," says Gemini. "And there's a strong emotion behind every real thought," answers Cancer. "But," says Leo, "there is a WILL behind each."

Unless one reaches the point of feeling that which is spoken or visualized, what metaphysicians call demonstration will not happen – or if it happens will be delayed. Experienced mental workers wait for the feeling of the "finished thing," for that is the prelude to birth – to demonstration. When one feels it, the event is very close.

The colors of Cancer are silver, violet and puce. Its gems are pearls. Its metal is silver. Its herbs are white poppies, cucumbers, green pepper, lettuce, water lilies, white lilies, water violets and water flag – plants that bloom at night or in water come under the domain of Cancer.

Careers that Cancer can excel at are parenting, family businesses, restaurants, delis, fast food and the food industry in general, child care centers, domestic real-estate, the silver industry, industries that deal with furnishings for the home, industries that deal with raising children, psychology – especially child psychology.

The most favorable periods of the year are June 21 – July 21 (Sun in Cancer); October 21 – November 21 (Sun in Scorpio); February 21 – March 21 (Sun in Pisces). The most favorable periods of the month are the days when the Moon is in Cancer, Scorpio or Pisces. The most favorable days of the week are Monday and Friday. The most favorable times of the day are during the hours of the Moon and when Cancer, Scorpio or Pisces is on the ascendant. (Hopefully it is understood that we mean this in a general way. No question that factors in the individual horoscope and the daily transits will modify these things considerably. But all things being equal, that is, if there are good aspects during the periods when the Sun or Moon is in Cancer, Scorpio or Pisces, these periods will tend to be more favorable than other periods with equally good aspects. A Monday with good aspects will be better than other days with equally good aspects.)

Reflexology points important to Cancer are the top part of the foot along the line of the fourth and fifth toes (both feet); the top part of the hand along the line of the fourth and fifth fingers (both hands), and the Achilles tendon of both feet where it merges into the calves. The stomach reflex in both hands and feet are also important. In the hands this reflex is right below the pad of the palm along the line of the second and third fingers in both hands. In the feet it is just below the ball of the foot along the line of the big toe.

Meditation for Cancer

"My feelings are a part of the universal mind. They represent the feelings of the Divine, feeling through me. My capacity to feel is infinite and I have access to all the higher moods and emotions. I abide in these emotions continually. I abide in the feelings of the Divine which are love, harmony, happiness, success, and peace. Those are the feelings that I cultivate and entertain. For I know that as I think and feel so is my future. If I don't like what I'm feeling at the moment I have the power to change it at will. I am as selective about my emotional states as I am about my clothing and accessories. I choose the best."

A Spiritual View of Leo

The deepest urge of Leo is to shine. To light up the dark caves and byways of life with its light and splendor.

In Leo the soul remembers that it is an individual light unto the world – a part of the universal light. As the master of Nazareth said, light was not made to be hidden under a bushel but to shine. In Leo the soul remembers this aspect of itself.

In Leo the soul remembers its essential royalty and majesty – a royalty and authority that is not conferred on it by "mortals" but which is innate to it. "Light rules the world," sayeth Leo. "This is in the nature of things. He who hath more Light ruleth me."

Leo instinctively feels and knows (though no one ever taught it this) that it is born to "rule" – born to shine; that he/she is something "special and unique" in the scheme of things. There is an innate sense of self-esteem and self-worth in the character which others trifle with at their own risk. The surest way to get into trouble with a Leo is to start belittling him/her or not giving him/her the respect and acknowledgment that the Leo feels is his/her due.

Light is neither a feeling (Cancer) nor a thought (Gemini). Light is the power with which we think and feel. Light is the power behind all psychological functioning – as well as physical functioning. Metaphysically speaking, light means intellectual and emotional "clarity." Clear perception of what is. Without light it is unsafe to start thoughts or feelings into motion. With light, it is not only safe but desirable. In Leo the soul discovers the power of light which takes it beyond the emotions of Cancer and beyond the logic of Gemini. For light is a superior principle.

In Leo the soul discovers the power of the will, which every ruler must have in order to rule. Real will is an awesome force – a dynamic spiritual force – much more dynamic than any of the

24

forces that the soul has been exploring in the first four signs. For, as Leo knows full well, the will can dominate the intellect (Gemini) and the emotions (Cancer).

"Where there is a will there is a way."

"In the will work and acquire if thou wouldst have thy heart's desire."

Part of the problem that intellectuals and psychologists have with the Leo type is precisely in this area that we have been discussing. Of what use is it to rail against the "illogic of the king" or the fact that your "feelings" at the moment don't coincide with his/her dictates when the Leo is functioning from a totally different dimension of things – the dimension of will?

The Leo type is generally not malicious and generally means well and generally exercises its will in line with what it considers to be some "greater good." And so the Leo will think in his/her heart, "Oh I know that you consider me illogical and unfeeling at the moment, but my will transcends your logic and your feelings. And though you don't think or feel as I do at the moment, presently you shall. For my will is creative. My will shall not only create a new reality but a new logic and psychology as well."

So powerful is the dimension of will – the arena in which our blessed Leos play – that it can even transform the sense of "I Am that I Amness" that the soul discovers in Aries. Through the will one can "be what one wills to be and do what one wills to do" (Aries); "have what one wills to have" (Taurus); "think what one wills to think" (Gemini); "feel what one wills to feel" (Cancer). "There is nothing more powerful than my will," says Leo.

And so the sign of Leo represents all the adventures and experiences that the soul acquires in its exploration of the will dimension. The Leo is king of the empire of his soul. He is not only a king of his own castle but also of anyone else "less willful and less illuminated" than he. How will he use this kingship? How will he use this authority? This is the challenge of Leo.

The evolved types unite their personal sense of will with the ONE WILL of the cosmos. They will only what the "Father in heaven wills" – they are "about the Father's business" – "doing the will of that which sent them into expression." These are the Christed ones, the true kings and authorities of this or any other world. Their true dominion is in the mental and psychological worlds where they exercise absolute authority. Their dominion here on the Earth – in the world of mortals – is also absolute but is exercised "indirectly." These are the great illuminators. The great channels of life and light into the world of mortals. Their will is unstoppable and invincible. It has dominion without any sense or feeling of "domination." They are not only bringers of light and life but also of joy and beauty. They restore the essential glamour and beauty of life on the Earth. They are of the race of "revelators" revealing new truths about reality and new good to those around them. For the nature of light is to reveal.

Without them life would be too drab and depressing to be worth living. Without them mortals would have destroyed each other long ago.

When such a being says, "I am the Way, the Truth and the Light" it is not a statement born of arrogance, but simply a statement of the nature of reality. A statement that is absolutely true to one who has risen to the level of WILL.

It seems to me that every Leo – even the lesser evolved – understands this and strives to express this truth in its own way – each according to its capacity. In the lesser evolved there tends to be a separation of its personal will from the "will of the Father" – and so the personal will "usurps," for a time, the true will. And even the personal will can be very powerful. Thus in these types there is a sense of arrogance and highhandedness. They can become tyrannical. Domineering. Overbearing. But the instant they make their "connection" with the Source of all will, they straighten out.

The Sun is the ruler of this sign, and if we meditate on the Sun

– its different phases, its nature, its central position in the solar system – we will understand our blessed Leos.

At its rising it is the resurrected king, the risen king, the mighty warrior – conqueror of death – banishing darkness, confusion, ignorance. Driving the "money changers from the temple." Asserting its lawful and legitimate dominion.

At midday it is the administrator king – perhaps a bit too hot, too strong, too dominating – exercising full authority in its domain. At the peak of its power and influence.

At sunset it is the lover.

At midnight it is the sacrificial king, dying so that others might live – sacrificing itself for the welfare – the greater good – of its subjects. For no mortal can take the full light of the Sun continually. This sacrificial aspect was always considered to be one of the privileges of royalty – reserved for royalty alone.

Any legitimate ruler is supposed to "reveal" the will and the plan for his subjects. He embodies in himself the national or group will and mediates between it and the ONE WILL. In this mediation lies the true art of government. Those who are closest to the perception of the Universal Will and who have the clearest perception of the evolutionary plan for a nation or group are the true rulers and kings of that group. In ancient times this was recognized and the king was considered to be BOTH a priest and a king. He was the supreme spiritual and temporal authority. (Until 1954 Tibet was the only nation that still governed itself in this way. But in ancient times this was quite common. It is still common in theocratic institutions – the Catholic Church, monasteries and "unofficially" among orthodox Jews. The supreme spiritual authority tends to be the supreme temporal authority.) The concept of the philosopher king is very similar to this.

The concept of the divine right of kings was based on this assumption – that the king was manifesting the Divine Will for the nation – leading it according to its special destiny. Of course, there were many so-called kings who ruled not by divine right, but by accident of birth, and who were not really fulfilling their true function. Thus, the concept of the divine right of kings fell into disrepute. But even today it is doubtful whether any ruler could govern effectively without the support of the priestly caste – whose job it is to discern the Universal Will-to-Good and carry out its plan. Kings and presidents still rule by divine right, only it is more "deeply disguised" today than it once was.

There is something about the power of light that makes it incompatible with the concept of "depression." Impossible to be in the "light" and be "depressed" at the same time. Light and sickness are also antagonistic concepts. Where there is light there is health. Where there is light there is joy. Where there is light there is warmth and love. Where there is light there is beauty. Where there is light there is harmony and power. And so the Leo type – instinctively – is a fun-lover. And Leo is the natural ruler of the Fifth House, the house of fun – fun in love, fun in creativity, entertainment, children, speculations and amusements.

"Life," says Leo, "is fun and games. We're here to have fun. To enjoy life."

If Leo had its way the world would be one gigantic amusement park. Or a gigantic play where everyone writes their own script and plays the role that they assign to themselves. All for the greater amusement and entertainment of all.

Perhaps they are right.

Leo is definitely concerned with the "fun aspect of life." The Greek god Dionysus (the god of wine, women and song) is a solar deity. And even Christianity concedes (underneath all the fire and brimstone and fear and guilt) that it is the Christ force that leads the soul to "rapture."

Careers most suitable for Leo are the arts, entertainment in all its forms, the theater, film, nightclubs, cabarets, amusement parks, amusement machines, slot machines, casinos, the stock market, gold mining or industries that deal with the mining and processing of gold, resorts (especially tropical-type resorts), industries dealing with solar energy, TV, film, jewelry (especially jewelry made of gold), athletics.

The Leo excels in any job where leadership qualities are called for. They function best, however, in their own business. They are not by nature team players, and this could create problems for them in the corporate or political arena where everything runs by consensus. They are "stars" by nature and need to find positions where this part of themselves can be expressed.

Leo's most favorable periods of the year are March 21 – April 21 (Sun in Aries); July 21 – August 21 (Sun in Leo); and November 21 – December 21 (Sun in Sagittarius). The most favorable times of a given month are when the Moon is in Aries, Leo or Sagittarius. The most favorable days of the week are Sunday and Tuesday. The most favorable hours of the day are the hours of the Sun and when Aries, Leo or Sagittarius is rising on the horizon. (Hopefully the reader will understand that all of this will be modified by individual factors in the personal horoscope and by the nature of the planetary transits. But what is being said here is that all things being equal, these periods will be more favorable for Leo than other periods. That is, if the aspects were equally good all around, these periods with good aspects would be more favorable than other periods with equally good aspects.)

The color of Leo is gold. Its metal is gold. Its gems are yellow diamonds, amber, and chrysolite. Its scents are frankincense, musk, orange blossom and lemon. Its herbs are sunflowers, poppies, chamomile, bay, eucalyptus, olive, cowslips, daffodils, dill, eye-bright, eglantine, helianthus, yellow lilies, marigolds and saffron. Most citrus fruits (and plants) are ruled by Leo.

Leo rules the heart and the back of the body in general. The reflexology points for Leo are just beneath the pads below the base of the fourth and fifth fingers of the left hand – the reflex to the heart – and just beneath the pad below the fourth and fifth toe on the left foot. These reflexes, plus the entire back of the body, should be massaged regularly – but especially when there are stressful transits. Also good to massage the fourth and fifth finger of the left hand and the fourth and fifth toe of the left foot. This energizes the heart area.

Meditation for Leo

"The same mighty will that willed the heavens and the Earth into being wills through me. For I am ONE with that Will now. I will only what 'my Father in heaven wills' – I desire only what the 'Father in heaven desires.' There are no two separated wills. Only one. Therefore my will is ONE with the ONE and there are no obstructions to it. It manifests for me in perfect and harmonious ways. One with this will, I am truly a light unto the world. I shine because it is my nature to shine – like the Sun and the stars. For I am made of the stuff of light. And in this light I perceive the All Good, All True and All Beautiful, and take my rightful place in executing its design here on Earth."

A Spiritual View of Virgo

In Virgo we find two important spiritual urges dominant in the character. One is the urge to serve – to be useful to others in a practical way. The second is an urge to technical mastery and perfection – almost to the point of mania.

All real spiritual urges have this sense of "compulsion" about them. A kind of overwhelming urgency that leaves the uninstructed mystified. But the mystery is easily cleared when we understand the origin of these "urges." These urges are the pressures of the Life Force pulsing through the being with invincible power. For the Life Force is not some blind irrational power. It is Intelligence manifesting according to intelligent patterns.

In Virgo, the soul – the medium through which the Life Power operates – has already absorbed all the lessons of Leo. It knows of its innate royalty, majesty and power. It has experienced all the pomp, ceremony, glamour, and fun of Leo and now it is ready for something more. Some new aspect of truth reveals itself to the soul. A new power and faculty is to be developed. For in Virgo the soul understands what rulership is all about. The king, for all his pomp and glamour, is nothing more than a figurehead unless he is serving the interests of his people. The greater the king (or queen) the greater the servant he/she is. Where the Leo is ready to die for others – to be the sacrificial king – Virgo wants to do something much more difficult. Virgo wants to live for them. To serve their interests. To be really useful. To really improve their quality of life. To minister to their physical needs.

To the Virgo mind there is nothing higher than service to others.

This Virgoan trait is often seen by others as "weakness." Nothing could be further from the truth. It is a serious misjudgment as these others soon learn. For in Virgo the urge to serve does not come from a "weakness in the ego" but from strength – not from "lack of self-esteem" but from a deeper sense of self-esteem. Service is seen as a natural privilege of royalty – the reason for its existence. Leadership itself is just another form of service.

"Who would rule best must serve best," says Virgo. "The best servant is the best ruler."

If we inquire as to what faculties are needed to provide excellence in service we find that there is a need to develop a technical mastery in the chosen field of service. One cannot be an effective servant if one is ignorant or doesn't know what one is doing. This is basic. So in Virgo the soul – motivated by its urge to serve and be useful – finds it necessary to develop technical perfection in his/her chosen field of service.

In order to technically master anything the faculty of analysis and discrimination is necessary. One must be able to break a project or task or area of knowledge down to its component parts – first to understand it and then to figure out the best ways of doing it. Breaking a task down to its component parts brings the analytical faculty into play. Choosing the best way of doing anything brings the discriminative faculty into play. Both of these faculties are highly developed in Virgo and Virgo intends to bring them to their ultimate development.

In Virgo, the soul has a very fresh memory of the perfection of the heavenly worlds. In heaven everything is perfect down to the minutest detail. Difficult for a mortal to even contemplate such perfection, but Virgo does it better than most. "Perfection is the way things SHOULD be," says Virgo. And they set about bringing this heavenly perfection down to earth – in their mind, their bodies and all the affairs of their lives. They are not "obsessive-compulsive" as they are often diagnosed. They are acting normally for a Virgo. They feel it is their mission to make things as perfect here on earth as they are in heaven.

Their "perfectionism" is really motivated by love – though others definitely misunderstand this. After all what is so romantic or loving about mastering the central nervous system? Or in knowing the vitamin content in every morsel of food? Where is the romance in doing the dishes absolutely perfectly? Isn't it more romantic to take your girlfriend to the local casino or nightclub for a night out on the town?

It seems that way, but it's not.

For in doing its job perfectly on the highest possible level the Virgo is showing its love. "My patients, my clients, my children, my boss, my stockholders, my loved ones deserve the best and I'm going to supply the best." They even behave this way sexually. What they lack in genuine passion they more than make up for in technical proficiency.

Virgo is love manifesting through service – on the dimension of Earth.

A Leo in love will take you to the theater or to the nightclubs and then make passionate love to you. A Taurus will take care of you as he/she would any "beloved possession." A Gemini will try to teach you things. The Cancerien will feed you and mother you. But the Virgo will serve you.

If you are loved by a Virgo, you might walk into your house one day and find that it is "immaculate" – spotless. Or, you might find vitamins in your medicine chest. Or, that your tax returns "mysteriously" got done. Or that your computer now works perfectly. The Virgo considers this kind of thing to be much more loving than bringing a bunch of useless flowers (which will only die in a few days anyway) or wasting money which could be used more effectively in your interest. In some countries this is considered the highest form of love. Words are cheap and tawdry. Sex is for the moment. Love talk is but for the moment and is generally insincere. But service – that is real, that remains, that is a concrete manifestation of love.

This need to be useful, to serve, is so strong that if a Virgo type is unemployed (even through circumstances beyond his/her control) they are miserable. And this is true even if they are wealthy and don't need to work. They LIKE to work. They are every employer's dream. The ultimate employee. Virgo is a much better employee than boss. As a boss he/she could definitely be too demanding, exacting and exasperating. Never satisfied. They tend to demand the same ultra-high standards of perfection of others that they demand of themselves. This of course is a mistake. For the Virgo temperament is the Virgo temperament and one cannot expect all people to share this view.

A typical – and classic – Virgo complaint runs something like this: "I hate this job, there's not enough to do!"

Like the Gemini the Virgo is intellectual but with some major differences. In Gemini the intellect is used to gather information indiscriminately. The Gemini is like the young boy hungry for knowledge who reads everything that he can get his hands on. Virgo is much more discriminating in its intellectual tastes. The only knowledge important to Virgo is knowledge that has "utility" – knowledge that can be put to use. Where Gemini is interested in words and ideas, Virgo is interested in the study of "concrete things" – the human body, the chemistry and nutritional value of food, the components of a computer, etc. In Virgo the power of the intellect is not just for communication or idle talk, but must be made to serve concrete ends.

Virgos excel in service-type industries. In the professions they are superb doctors, nurses, nutritionists, dieticians, reflexologers, masseuses, hygienists, psychic healers, herbalists, chiropractors, veterinarians (especially for small animals). In fact the entire health industry is good for them. They are also excellent architects and draftsmen. In the business world they are super secretaries, administrative assistants, accountants, computer programmers/engineers, personnel officers in any industry. Employment agencies are excellent. Any profession that requires fine, painstaking detail work is excellent for the Virgo type.

Virgo's most favorable periods of the year are April 21 – May 21 (Sun in Taurus); August 21 – September 21 (Sun in Virgo); and

December 21 – January 21 (Sun in Capricorn). Its most favorable periods of the month are when the Moon is in Taurus, Virgo or Capricorn. The most favorable day of the week is Wednesday. The most favorable periods of the day are Mercury's hours and when Taurus, Virgo or Capricorn is rising.

Virgo's colors are earth tones, ocher and orange. Its metal is quicksilver. Its gem is hyacinth. Its herbs and plants are wheat, rye, millet, oats, barley, caraway, fennel, carrots, celery, parsley, anise, valerian, woodbine, and skullcap.

Virgo rules the intestines and the digestive system of the body in general – and if we meditate on these functions we will understand the special power of the sign. The reflexology points important for Virgo are the lower central portion of both feet, above the heel, the reflexes to the intestines. These should be massaged regularly but especially when there are stressful transits.

Meditation for Virgo

"I am he (or she) who was created in the flawless image and likeness of God. And there were no imperfections in that image. And therefore there are no imperfections in my image or body except those that I created for myself by false thinking, fear and worry. I identify with this perfect image now. I recognize it now. I embody and express it now. I am the health of the One Spirit. Every cell and organ and function of my body was perfectly formed and visualized by a mind far transcending my own. I am ONE with that mind now and I see and feel every cell, organ and function of my body in perfect and flawless operation now. I am centered and unmoved in this image now."

A Spiritual View of Libra

In Libra the soul discovers another of its infinite powers and capacities. The power of love. The power of beauty. The importance of human (and other) relationships to its well-being.

True, this love is still "human," still "personal," still directed to specific "objects" and a far cry from the real spiritual love – changeless, unconditional, eternal – that the soul will discover in Pisces. Nevertheless it is far more developed, far more exalted, over the possessive kind of love of Taurus and the instinctual – gut feeling – kind of love of Cancer.

If you talk to a Virgo he/she will say, "Being useful is what life is all about." A Libra will think quite differently. "Love is what it's all about – love and romance and relationships." They will even take it a step further and assert that "self-knowledge only comes through relationships – there is no other way."

And so it is for them.

In order to realize its ideal of service the Virgo needed to develop intellectual faculties that were basically separative – the powers of analysis and discrimination. Diligent, honest and sincere though Virgo was in performing service to others, somewhere in its development it discovers something. It cannot realize its ideal of service in any meaningful way without cooperation from others. What good is it to patients if all the doctors are specialists and all the nurses the best in their field but there is inharmony between them – if they don't cooperate with each other, if there is not right human relations between all the parties performing the service? The result is a shambles.

Not enough to have technical mastery of a field. For without right human relationships the mastery cannot even be brought into play.

At about this point the Virgo is getting ready for the experience of Libra.

For now the Virgo has to take the same intellectual power that was directed to acquiring technical mastery and apply it in a new and different way. Now he/she will have to apply it to the art of relationship – the art of getting along with others – the art of obtaining human cooperation in one's endeavors.

This, it seems to me, is the essence of Libra. It is MORE than just love and romance (though this is a major part of it). It is "clear thinking" – hard, analytical, rational thought – applied to relationships.

Libra's thought and genius is "unitive" – "integrative." It looks for the things that "bring people together" where in Virgo it was looking at the things that tend to separate people. The Virgo notices differences, the Libra looks for similarities – for the similarities are the points where varied types of people can meet and cooperate.

Many people think that Libra is "naive and blind to other people's faults," therefore love is easy to them. But this isn't precisely true. The Libra is very conscious of your faults – remember it is a post-Virgo sign – but will love you anyway in spite of them. How does it manage to do this? By focusing attention on the good points – the points of mutual harmony, the points of mutual agreement. Here is revealed the secret of the "blessed ties that bind" – the secret of successful relationships, the secret of social grace, charm and popularity, the secret of all diplomacy and cooperation between people. This is Libra's great gift to the world. And entire religions have been based on little more than this.

In Virgo the soul was content to render service that was, from the technical point of view, the ultimate of perfection. But in Libra the soul teaches a new revelation – not only must the service be performed with the utmost technical skill, but it must be performed beautifully, gracefully, lovingly. It must become a thing of beauty. A living work of art. The soul has entered an entirely new dimension – the dimension of art. From the technician it becomes the artist. (The fact that Virgo precedes Libra gives us some indication of what real art is all about. The artist is the technician par excellence and MORE. Technical proficiency should precede art in the natural order of development as described by the zodiac.) In Libra the soul remembers its essential and innate beauty. That it was created by beauty, for the purposes of beauty. It recognizes it about itself and about others also.

It remembers its essential right to it – its right and obligation to express beauty and to be beauty. And this perception is the basis of all art.

Libra therefore is always the artist, either consciously or unconsciously. It is the artist in its relationships, in its romances, in painting, in music, in design – and especially with one's self. The Libra sees its own body – its physical image, its personality – to be an ever-evolving work of art and beauty. Thus the interest in clothes and jewelry and fine surroundings. It is not so much a matter of egoic satisfaction with Libra as it is with other signs. Libra is simply the artist and every medium – including the body, the home, one's clothing, one's social manner – is a valid medium for the expression of its highest concepts of beauty, harmony and grace.

The power of beauty is awesome. No one has ever explored it to its ultimate – and probably no one ever will. For we are dealing with an infinite principle – an aspect of the Divine – and there are no limits to it. One can easily see why so many choose to devote their lives to this. There are things a lot worse that we devote ourselves to.

Libra's quest to create and express beauty is – on its deepest levels – motivated by love. Where there is beauty love spontaneously arises. Impossible to love something that is truly ugly (if such a thing could exist anywhere except in distorted human thought). Beauty and love go together. In cases where love seems to exist for something or someone that is "superficially speaking" ugly, if you analyze a bit deeper, you will find that there is usually a perception of beauty beneath the appearance – a beauty of soul, a beauty of manner, a beauty of thought, a beauty of character, a moral beauty of some kind. Libra, being endowed with remembrance of the essential beauty of the world, looks for beauty everywhere – and generally finds it. And this is the key to falling in love. The key to real romance.

Beauty is the perception of truth as felt by the heart. When it is perceived by the rational faculties we call it truth. Truth and beauty are twin sides of a coin. If a thing is true it is also beautiful. If it is beautiful it is true.

A universe unillumined by the genius of Libra is starkly unthinkable – and so we owe these types a lot. It seems to me that it is the alchemy of art that mainly differentiates a "love affair" from "romance." Both types of relationship involve sex and passion, but a romance involves aesthetic beauty as well. In the first case there is the relief of mutual need and some fun (nothing wrong with that); in the second case there is art involved, there is a creation of something beautiful. The artistic or fantasy faculties are called into play. Deeper centers of the mind are at work – MORE of the being is involved in a romance than in a mere love affair. One's higher genius is called into play with romance.

Sex, of itself, is very uninteresting to a Libra. Sex is only interesting to them as a part of something larger. The sexual act, the scene of the sexual act, the circumstances of sex must be beautiful and aesthetically pleasing in some way. It is doubtful whether you would learn much about sexual behavior from a Libra if you strapped electrodes to its organs with a bunch of strangers "objectively" recording their findings.

A Libra can appreciate sex as art – erotica. And it can appreciate sex as one of the ways that lovers relate to each other. But sex as sex, or as some impersonal biological function, seems low and degrading to them.

One can easily understand Libra's preoccupation with love and beauty and social matters. It's a powerful toy. Art changes the destiny of nations. A beautiful woman can launch a thousand ships. Beauty is a tremendous healing force. "And love," says Libra, "makes the world go round."

"Where would incarnating souls find bodies if there were no physical attraction between man and woman causing them to unite and marry?" says Libra.

"My genius," says Libra, "facilitates the love force, and lifts the minds of mortals to higher things. Without me there is no harmony and if there is no harmony there is no health."

"Beauty is the health of a soul."

Relationship is so important to Libra that they will prefer a "bad or painful relationship" to the alternative of NO relationship. This is not true of all signs, but in Libra it is definitely true.

The pain of a bad relationship is much more preferable to them than the absolute devastation of NO relationship. In a bad relationship – painful though it can be – there is still scope for them to exercise their genius. There are things that can be learned. Their skills can be sharpened and honed. But in the state of no relationship, their whole genius and gift is idle – unused – without a medium for its expression. And this is unacceptable to Libra – a kind of slow death.

A Libra who is not involved in some romance is as miserable as a Virgo who is unemployed or a Taurus who is broke. A very serious matter to them.

The symbol of Libra is the scales. This indicates to us that beauty is balance; that perfect love means – by definition – perfect justice; that good relationships require a balance of the needs of both parties; that both parties are equally important in the relationship (though they are not the same). The scales of Libra make an interesting meditation.

Libra excels in the fine arts, fashion (either as model or as designer), hosts and hostesses, diplomacy, fine furniture, interior decorating or design, cosmetology, jewelry and personal accessories, matchmaking (either on the personal level or on a corporate level), go-betweens, party planners and caterers, hair styling, manicurists, antiques. Any industry dealing with enhancing beauty, whether it be of the physical image or of the environment is excellent for Libra. If Saturn is strong in the chart Libra could excel in the legal profession or as a judge.

Libra's color is jade green. Its metal is copper. Its scents are rose and vanilla. Its gems are emeralds, chrysolite, coral, carnelian, jade, opal, quartz, and white marble. Its herbs and plants are lemon-thyme, roses, violets, vanilla, potato, almond, apple blossoms, and peach blossoms.

The most favorable periods of the year for Libra are May 21 – June 21 (Sun in Gemini); September 21 – October 21 (Sun in Libra); January 21 – February 21 (Sun in Aquarius). The most favorable periods of the month are when the Moon is in Gemini, Libra or Aquarius. The most favorable days of the week are Friday and Monday. The most favorable periods of the day are the hours of Venus and when Gemini, Libra or Aquarius is rising. (These will be modified by individual factors in the horoscope and the daily transits of the planets. But what we're saying here is that all things being equal these periods will be more favorable than other periods with equivalent aspects. Thus a Friday with good aspects will be more favorable for Libra than a Tuesday with equally good aspects.)

Reflexology points important to Libra are at the bottom of the pad (mound of Saturn) beneath the middle finger of both hands and just below the ball of the foot along the line of the middle toes – both feet. These are the reflexes to the kidneys. These should be regularly massaged, but especially when the transits are stressful. Hip massage is also very beneficial for Libra.

Meditation for Libra

"Love and beauty are not separated from me. They are actual aspects of the One Mind that created the heavens and the Earth and which created me. I am one with that mind now. I am one with that Spirit now. Therefore I am One with all the love and beauty there is. Love and beauty are actual energies and forces and I open my mind to these forces now. I abide in love and beauty continually. I love and I am loved. I was created beautiful by beauty. I express it in all areas of my life in my body, my thoughts, my environment, and relationships. I am love. I am beauty. And presently it shall manifest in my experience."

A Spiritual View of Scorpio

When the soul entered the gate of Libra it thought it had found the ultimate meaning and purpose of life – love. Beauty. Beauty taught by love. Romance. Harmony and peace between humans. Happy human relationships. But somewhere in its sojourn through this paradise it discerns the snake and the scorpion. Indeed it has been bitten more than once.

If there is nothing else but love, if love alone matters, if God is love, why is there so much suffering? Why is romance so painful? Why doesn't love last? Why do we seem to keep hurting those that we supposedly love?

And another painful reality hits Libra. This marriage I'm into – happy though it is – cannot last. It is doomed to end. Death will end it. Death – the ultimate separation – has power over my happiness.

This beauty of form that I have cultivated, that I have made my personal work of art, is also fleeting. Beauty is like a rose. It blooms for a period and then fades and dies. How tragic! How sad!

Could it be that death and old age are stronger forces than love and beauty? Could a God of love decree an end to love? How cruel! How inhuman! Why is it that no matter how hard I try there are barriers between my lover and me? Why is it that so many people reject love, almost resent it, attack it bitterly? Why are there so many people who resent and attack beauty?

What's going on here?

Nothing serious. The soul is about ready for the experience of Scorpio. For the soul is beginning to see clearly the unregenerate elements of itself and others; elements that cannot be dealt with by "diplomacy and charm" – other powers and faculties have to be developed. New understandings have to surface. The soul is confronted with the problem of "evil" and the soul will have to become the warrior. Libra enters willingly into this because it realizes that its ideal of love cannot manifest unless all the barriers and obstructions to it are overcome – destroyed. In the name of love does Libra enter the experience of Scorpio.

Scorpio is the ultimate warrior. One could not ask for a more dangerous adversary or a more loyal friend. The Scorpio has a "stick-to-it-iveness" that Aries, the other warrior of the zodiac, doesn't dream of. The Scorpio also has a subtlety and depth – a mastery of secret, invisible forces – of which Aries as yet is unaware. Besides, those who love best are the best warriors. Scorpio, which is a progression of Libra, understands what love is all about and instinctively knows what should and should not be destroyed.

The Aries could tend to destroy indiscriminately when the lust of battle is upon him. Not so the Scorpio. The Scorpio will be selectively destructive – destroying only that which cannot be useful to him, leaving intact the elements that might come in handy later on. Scorpio's passions are controlled passions – passions focused by and under the control of the ego. Passions intensified to their highest point are one of the tools by which Scorpio attains its ends – either of construction or destruction.

The laser beam – which is light intensified to incredible degrees of brightness – is an apt symbol for Scorpio.

Scorpio has this innate power to concentrate – focus – and penetrate. If you've ever looked at their eyes you'll know what I mean. One can tell a Scorpio by the eyes.

In Scorpio the soul remembers its power to transform and regenerate; that it has the power to "die and be born again;" that it has the power to "invent and re-invent itself" as it wills; that it has total power – unconditional power – over all conditions and circumstances – creation and uncreation.

The Scorpio is essentially a soul in revolt. It is, quite frankly, a bit disgusted with the social toadying of Libra. It sees – very clearly – how certain elements in society use the Libra's need for social acceptance to enslave it against Libra's better interests. These coercive forces are invisible – subtle – but very real nevertheless. There is no one person or group that one can point one's finger at doing the coercing, but it is there nevertheless – in the unregenerate elements of the group unconscious. The Scorpio realizes also that it – until it awakened – was also a tool of these coercive, unconscious forces. It is a bitter pill to swallow. But now the soul decides to "take control" of these powers – to wield and manipulate them itself instead of being manipulated by them. In order to do so, it must first study and understand them – hence the interest in occultism and occult power.

If we ask ourselves what the primary prerequisites are for the process of transformation whether it be of one's self, one's environment, one's career or any material condition, we find that there is a need for silence and secrecy – a need to "come out from among them and be separate," a need for one-pointedness, total concentration, a need to die and in the dying overcome the fear of death (which is usually what keeps the soul in some undesirable condition) and then be reborn into the new and self-created condition.

The Scorpio is not after some temporary superficial, cosmetic change. This might have satisfied it in Libra where everything is a matter of form and surface. But not now. It wants fundamental change. This desire is normal and natural to the soul at this stage. If we meditate on the process that transpires when the seed becomes a plant or when a caterpillar becomes a butterfly or a tadpole becomes a frog, we will get some insight into the kind of change that Scorpio desires deep, deep down. It is this that motivates its behavior.

Sex and death are probably the most potent transforming powers that we know of. Sex means the "union of opposites." When this really happens (we're not talking about "pseudo-sex," or nervous reactions that people pass off as sex) a transformation takes place – there is a death and new birth. This happens on the physical plane and also on all the other dimensions of being. When two opposite ideas or concepts are mated, both of these ideas "die" and a new, synthetic concept is born – something very often radically different from the initial opposites. This is the basis of the dialectic technique in philosophy. When a man and woman truly mate, the "me" and the "you" "die" and it becomes "we" – something new, something radically different – transformation.

Scorpio finds sex much more interesting than romance. Very unlike the Libra. Sex is real; romance is fantasy. Sex is an act capable of producing "living life forms" – bodies. The best romance can muster up is some poetry, art and perhaps a sonata or two. In Libra sex is either art or romance; in Leo it is another way to have fun; in Cancer it is the mechanism by which it can exercise its genius of building a family – procreation; in Scorpio it is power.

In Scorpio the soul discovers many new dimensions of the sex energy – and many different uses for it. There is a lot more to this than most people realize. For as Scorpio discovers in his subterranean researches, the sex principle (or polarity, which was traditionally the more polite way to describe it) goes "way up to the Highest Heavens" and can be used to create "other bodies" – mental and spiritual bodies that are immune to the processes of death. In Scorpio the soul first becomes aware of the "possibility" of immortality – and many other soul faculties as well. These are the powers that will enable it through practice and expertise to totally transform itself, its environment and conditions – and if it so wills even the world. These are the powers by which the "snake can grow wings and become an eagle."

If Scorpio seems promiscuous to the "Mrs. Grundy mentality" it is because Scorpio does not see any "evil" in sex. The Scorpio has learned what libido is and where it comes from and does not feel the taboos imposed on it are real or legitimate. To Scorpio, sexual expression is only one of the various expressions of the life force – and as lawful as any other.

In Scorpio we find the fulfillment of Libra. In Scorpio we see the solution to the sorrows of Libra. No longer need there be a separation from those that we love – no, not even death can separate the regenerated or recreated one from the object of his/her love. No longer can society create taboos and obstructions to real romance, for the Scorpio knows how to change society – break the obstruction or withdraw from society – if he feels it's necessary.

Careers good for Scorpio are surgery, occultism, scientific, medical or occult research, sex therapy, morticians, undertakers, the military, nuclear medicine, the nuclear energy industry, tax and bill collectors, plumbers, plumbing supply, life insurance, estate attorneys, estate planners, slaughterhouses, dealing with other people's money, making profits for others, managing other people's money, bankers, radiologists, blood testers, blood takers, intelligence officers. Any job requiring an ability to "penetrate into secret places" – to see beneath the surface of things – is ideal for Scorpio.

Scorpio's color is red-violet – burgundy. Its metals are iron, steel and radium. Its scents are sandalwood and banana. Its gems are topaz, malachite, and bloodstone. Its herbs and plants are pulsalla, charlock, leek, banana plants, peanuts, sandalwood, green peas, woad, and wormwood.

During the year Scorpio's most favorable periods are June 21 – July 21 (Sun in Cancer); October 21 – November 21 (Sun in Scorpio); February 21 – March 21 (Sun in Pisces). The most favorable periods in a given month are when the Moon is in the signs of Cancer, Scorpio or Pisces. The most favorable day of the week is Tuesday. The most favorable times of a given day are the hours of Mars, and when Cancer, Scorpio or Pisces is rising. (These statements are often radically modified by individual factors in the horoscope and by the daily transits. But what we're trying to say here is that all things being equal these periods, days and hours are more favorable than other times. A day when the Moon is in Pisces and the overall aspects are good will be more favorable for Scorpio than a day when the Moon is in Leo and the aspects are good. A Tuesday with good aspects will be more favorable than a Wednesday with good aspects.)

Reflexology points important to Scorpio are the wrists of both hands, the ankles of both feet, and the arch of both feet where it merges into the heel. Regular colonics are excellent for Scorpio as well.

Meditation for Scorpio

"I am an immortal being of light. I am the light that shineth in the darkness. I am the power of light amid the appearances of darkness and chaos. In this light I create the self that I will to be, the conditions and circumstances that I wish to live in. What I create here in the secrecy and silence of my self shall someday be shouted from the housetops of manifestation. For I am only exercising my lawful and legitimate 're-creative power' which I am heir too. I am silent about it. I do not deny my inner work during the course of the day. And lo and behold I watch it come to pass."

A Spiritual View of Sagittarius

The Scorpio experience was the ending of a major epoch in the soul's experience. And like all seeming endings it is only the beginning of something new.

When the serpent of Scorpio has grown wings (when the kundalini or libido has been liberated, elevated and exalted, raised to its divine status, united with its source) the eagle can fly. The soul has acquired the power to function in various dimensions. It is not limited by time, place and circumstance but knows itself to be superior to all of these. When the eagle starts to fly – to travel, to explore – it is ready for the experience of Sagittarius.

If Scorpio could be called the transformation phase of snake to eagle – the process by which a snake (a creature of the lower regions of the Earth) becomes, through the process of metamorphosis, an eagle (a king of the high places of the air) – then Sagittarius could be called the "eagle in flight," the eagle beginning its new life as a new creature.

The first major difference between the eagle and the snake is the difference in VISION – in perspective. No question that the eagle can cover more territory, can see more, know more, and has a radically bigger perspective of things than the snake does crawling on the ground – under the heel of man and beast.

This larger vision of reality – the expansion of perspective – is one of the main characteristics of the Sagittarian nature. "The limits and boundaries which have held us back formerly are no longer valid," says Sagittarius. "Reality is not what we have formerly believed! There are many mansions in the Father's house and I will explore them all!" A very difficult attitude for "earthbound" creatures to comprehend or to cope with.

In Sagittarius the soul is preoccupied with the gaining of this larger vision, and what fun it is to acquire! True, many, many flights – each ever larger and perhaps more dangerous – will be needed, for even an eagle in flight cannot traverse all space at once. But who cares! There is nothing more important than gaining the vision and sharing it with others.

With this vision – this enlargement of perspective – comes an unquenchable optimism. Optimism always accompanies an enlargement of perspective. Pessimism comes from a constriction of perspective – a narrowing of the vision.

Sagittarius is the questing soul – the eternal sannyasin – but with new and enlarged faculties. It sees more because it has become more. And with each "journey" it expands its vision – its conceptions, its horizons and its knowledge. And it will keep making these journeys until this part of itself is sated. No use to tell it at this stage to "settle down," "stop running around," "grow some roots." Sagittarius is the "arrow forever in flight – forever winging to its mark." It hasn't arrived there yet, but there is no question that it shall and it will.

Sagittarius is the soul in quest for wisdom. And this is the way that wisdom – higher knowledge, Truth – is attained. By physical and mental journeys. By ACTUAL observation and experience of new and unknown territories.

Very often the Sagittarian will not tarry long enough in one place to "reap his reward" – for the reaping of the rewards is not really his interest. When it comes time to reap the reward he is off to a new adventure. The quest itself is the rapture – not the rewards of the quest.

The image of a young child in a vast department store comes to me. The child is given "free access" to all parts of the giant store – to all departments and sections. The store is loaded with every conceivable desirable item – everything a child could want or ask for. The child goes to one section but does not take anything from it – though he is permitted to have and take anything that he wills. He fears – perhaps rightfully so – that he will find better goods in the next section and doesn't want to cumber himself with possessions that might block him from taking something better elsewhere in the store. After all, his capacity is only so much. There is only so much that he can carry. So in his initial wanderings in the store he is content to just explore – to see what it contains. After this is done, he might decide to take some of the precious gifts there – but only after he knows what the store contains and what is available.

The store is the wisdom dimension – or the universe. The child is the soul in its Sagittarius phase. He is just exploring. The goods in the store might or might not interest him – but what really interests him is the fact that the store IS – it exists, it is there, and it is open to all those who have need of its goods.

Sagittarius is more interested in letting the world know about its existence than in "carting off its treasures" to the world. "I have no need to hoard," says Sagittarius, "for I know the way and I can always return to the Father's mansion and take whatever I need when I need it. But there are others on the Earth who do not even know of the existence of such a mansion and so I will carry the message to them so that those in need can come to the store and be sated and fulfilled."

A true attitude of wealth. A true consciousness of affluence.

Sagittarius is the natural ruler of religion, philosophy and metaphysics. For these are the tools that the soul needs to enter and to explore the "higher dimensions of mind." Very difficult to understand religion – the attitude of religion – without this larger vision of reality.

It rules institutions of higher learning and on the physical plane it rules foreign travel. Institutions of higher learning put the soul in contact with its mental wealth.

The fact that Jupiter – the planetary ruler of Sagittarius – is BOTH the ruler of wealth and opulence as well as the ruler of religion, philosophy, metaphysics, and higher learning is a message to us about where the true origin of all wealth is – where wealth comes from, how it is manifested. Wealth originates in mind – the higher mind. And anyone who "unites with this mind" properly cannot experience any "lack or poverty," for these things are alien to this mind.

The extravagance and generosity of Sagittarius comes from this mind – which knows of its infinite wealth and knows that it can "well afford" to give, that its resources could never be depleted.

There are three levels of Sagittarius. The younger soul tends to be attracted by the "travel-exploration" dimension. They tend to be "jet setters" – living (or trying to live) the jet set lifestyle. I find it interesting that even Sagittarians of limited means – they work at minimum wage jobs – still somehow, miraculously, manage to travel a lot. They find ways.

The second, more advanced level of Sagittarius, is the academic – the professor, the keeper and dispenser of higher knowledge. The publisher also falls in this category.

The third and highest level of Sagittarian expression is the Priest-Rabbi-Imam-Minister-Guru. Sagittarius is the natural Priesthood of the planet – in its highest expression. They teach the people the spiritual laws. They mediate between man and the Divine. They bring the Divine Energy into the world. This is the true purpose of all the various forms of worship that we see. Without these practices, the Divine Energy wouldn't come in as it should. Bad though things seem in the world, a reduction in this Divine Energy would make things even worse.

Careers that the Sagittarius excels at are priest, minister, rabbi, philosopher, metaphysician, theologian; the travel industry; college professor or any profession dealing with the industry of higher education or religion; publishing in all its phases but especially book or textbook publishing; writing and teaching about travel, religion, philosophy, theology; foreign affairs in government or industry; international banking; horse breeding and horseback riding; jockey or wrangler, dude ranches; law, but better with the philosophical aspects of the law; international liaison; tin workers, tin mining, the tin industry.

The most favorable periods of the year for Sagittarius are November 21 – December 21 (Sun in Sagittarius); March 21 – April 21 (Sun in Aries); July 21 – August 21 (Sun in Leo). The most favorable periods of any given month are when the Moon is in Aries, Leo or Sagittarius.

The most favorable days of the week are Thursday and Friday. The most favorable times of the day are the hours of Jupiter and when Aries, Leo or Sagittarius is rising. (This is definitely modified by individual factors in the horoscope and by the daily transits. But what we're saying is that "all things being equal" these periods will be better than other periods with equivalent aspects. A Thursday with good planetary aspects will tend to be more favorable for Sagittarius than a Saturday with equivalent aspects. Sun in Leo with good aspects will be better than Sun in Virgo with good aspects.)

The color of Sagittarius is blue. Its metal is tin. Its gems are turquoise and carbuncle. Its scents are myrrh and jasmine. Its plants and herbs are jasmine, myrrh, betony, balsam, banyan, feather-few, and mallows.

Sagittarius rules the thighs, the part of the body which provides the power to travel or walk long distances – also the part of the body with which we ride a horse, man's earliest instrument of "long-distance travel." The thighs should be massaged regularly, but especially when there are stressful planetary transits. Reflexology points for Sagittarius are the lines from the fourth and fifth toes – just beneath the ball of the right foot. The lines beneath the fourth and fourth fingers of the right hand, just beneath the pad of the hand, are also important. These too should be regularly massaged.

Meditation for Sagittarius

"I am an immortal being of light. I am one with God and in perfect union and harmony with the universe. The wisdom of

God – which is cosmic – is ever flowing through my consciousness. It is flowing right now, illuminating my path, making straight the way and leading me unto every desirable thing. I am open and receptive to this cosmic wisdom now. All is well. Wisdom is flowing through my financial consciousness. Wisdom is flowing through my love consciousness. Wisdom is flowing through every cell and organ of my body – healing and purifying and strengthening me. Wisdom is flowing through my social consciousness. Wisdom is flowing through my sexual consciousness. All is well."

A Spiritual View of Capricorn

Among astrologers it's a toss-up as to which signs are most "difficult" to understand. Some say it is Pisces. Some say Scorpio. Others say Capricorn. For sure, Capricorn is in the top three of "most complex" signs.

Capricorn's ruler is Saturn, said by some to be the most "materialistic" of planets – and yet Capricorn is the natural ruler of the Tenth House – the most "elevated" point in the horoscope. Capricorn seems to us to be the most ambitious, materialistic of signs and yet it is said that it is the sign of cosmic consciousness.

It is in materialistic Capricorn that Christians celebrate the birth of the Christ – the ultimate in spirituality and non-worldliness. Saturn's metal is lead and yet its natives seem to have a lot of gold. Capricorns are noted for discipline and self-denial and yet one of its symbols is the cornucopia.

How are we to make heads or tails of this?

First off let's remember that Capricorn is a post-Sagittarius sign. The soul in Sagittarius has already acquired its vision. It has traveled and explored the known universe. It has known the power of love and romance in Libra. It has known rapture in Leo. But in Capricorn the soul remembers something new – its duty to life as a conscious soul. It remembers that it is here for a reason – it has work to do, a specific mission here in matter, here in the world of mortals.

Capricorn feels that there's plenty of time for love and rapture and exploration of "higher worlds" after death. But while it is here on Earth, it is here to DO something, to achieve something, to manifest its part of the vision – of the plan (that it has discerned in Sagittarius) – here on Earth. It remembers its DUTY. Its RESPONSIBILITY to the universe. It longs to fulfill it.

It considers its duty here on Earth to be the highest spirituality. Caesar doing his job properly is God on Earth. There is no dichotomy in the mind of Capricorn between Caesar and God. It was divinely ordained that God rules in heaven and that Caesar rules on Earth. And if it was divinely ordained then Caesar and his domain could not be "evil" or unspiritual. Capricorn is very ready to concede dominion of the heavens to the powers that exist there – nor do the higher developed ones deny such powers. "What I can see, touch and feel – that which I can measure with my senses and my intellect – that is my domain and there I shall rule," says Capricorn. "Let the invisible powers rule in the invisible, but in the known realms I shall rule."

In Sagittarius the soul was an "explorer of the heights" – a traveler, an eternal pilgrim. In Capricorn the soul wants to "establish itself" there. Set up housekeeping there. Live there in safety and security. Go up and come down as it wills. And this is a whole different ball game.

Now the soul will have to create structures – form, a system, an organization. For it is one thing to discover wells of living water far from civilization and quite another to bring the water to the "marketplace" so that all can drink in an orderly, harmonious way. The building of pipelines becomes necessary. A marketing organization is needed. The cooperation of others is necessary and the assent of society must be gotten.

Material structures are the forms through which the spiritual vision of Sagittarius is manifest on Earth. And so it takes the genius of Capricorn to achieve this. Administrative intelligence. Management skills. Order. Scheduling. Budgets. Goal setting. The best, most cost-efficient forms to get the job done. Politicking. Patience. Hard work. Endurance. Stick-to-it-iveness. And sometimes, arm twisting.

In Sagittarius the soul had its head in the sky; in Capricorn the soul's mind is definitely on Earth – and its nose is to the grind-stone. In Sagittarius the soul was taking a "spiritual initiation." In Capricorn it is taking a "corporate initiation." It is going to see how well its wisdom "works" in the world. It is a transition from theory to actual practice – and this is one of the great "abysses" that every person faces.

In Capricorn the soul sort of remembers that it is "normal" – in the natural order of things – for Spirit to materialize, for ideas to take on a body. In religion we see this in the form of a church or temple or a ministry of many, many churches. In economics an idea quickly becomes a corporation, a business enterprise; in art, a painting or piece of music. Ideas – if they are real – naturally take on a form. And certainly there could not be anything "evil" about this tendency. It's natural.

However, opposite faculties and talents are involved in the materialization of Spirit. First the idea must be discerned and discovered – worked out on the mental plane – conceptually. This requires a sort of idealism – an unearthliness, a need to be "absent from the body and present with the Lord," a "head in the sky" kind of orientation. But once this happens, other faculties come into play, other forces set to work – the forces of Capricorn. And once the idea is manifest all kinds of new factors are introduced that were never envisioned by the "visionary" who dreamed it up in the first place. Once you have an organization, money becomes a priority. People have to be paid. Supplies have to be bought. Jobs have to be allotted. A hierarchy – official or unofficial – is created. Competition for place and position enters into the picture. And sometimes all of these "side issues" become so passionate that the original idea – intent – is totally obscured. And here is the challenge of Capricorn. To maneuver through the whirlwinds of matter – dealing with all these forces – and yet still make sure that the idea-vision is manifest properly. A difficult assignment, but Capricorn is uniquely qualified to handle it.

Capricorn loves to manage things – to be in charge. It feels that management is its particular genius and its duty. And that only he/she stands between society and chaos.

We mentioned earlier that it is not enough for Capricorn to

"get to the top." It wants to get there safely and to abide there in security. Getting there safely means a mastery of the territory to be traversed. It means planning. Conscious effort. It means a study of the past – the solutions that have traditionally worked – and a selection of the way that is best. Capricorn reveres tradition for various reasons – one of the most important of them being that tradition represents man's past solutions to similar problems. Tradition represents solutions and techniques that "work" and that have stood the "test of time." This is the ultimate "acid test" for a Capricornian evaluation. "Does it (the product, system, theory, social form, etc.) work? Has it been tested? Has it stood the test of time?"

Understandably this prudence – which is really a desire for safety and security – tends to make for an ingrained conservatism. For, nothing new – by definition – has "stood the test of time."

On the other hand, knowing that the safety and security of others depend on him/her, this Capricornian prudence is understandable. But if insisted on too radically it would effectively arrest any progress. Nothing new could get born.

Capricorn does not see this as any particular tragedy. It is not really interested in the "new." The Capricorn wants to master the "tried and true." "Mastering an existing tradition is hard enough," says Capricorn, "I don't really have time to go off exploring new ways or techniques. My priority is to master what already exists."

Capricorns excel in the corporate "hierarchical world." They are managers, administrators, executives par excellence. Government and public service appeals to them also. Real estate, architecture, politics, jurisprudence, mining, orthopedics, chiropractic and crystallography are excellent fields. Old-age homes and industries dealing with services to older people, the watch and clock industry, the coal industry are also ruled by Capricorn.

Capricorn's most favorable periods of the year are April 21 –

May 21 (Sun in Taurus); August 21 – September 21 (Sun in Virgo); December 21 – January 21 (Sun in Capricorn). Its most favorable periods of the month are when the Moon is in Taurus, Virgo or Capricorn. The most favorable day of the week is Saturday. The most favorable hours of the day are the hours of Saturn and when Taurus, Virgo or Capricorn is rising. (This is of course modified by factors in the individual horoscope and by the transiting planets. But all things being equal these periods will be more favorable than other periods with equivalent aspects.)

Capricorn's colors are indigo and black. Its metal is lead. Its stones are onyx, jet and moonstone. Its plants and herbs are poplar, plantain, pine, ebony, black poppies, quince, nightshade, henbane, magnolia and dock.

Capricorn rules the knees. These, along with the spine (but not directly on the spine – the muscles just to the left and the right of it), should be massaged regularly, but especially when there are stressful aspects.

Reflexology points important for Capricorn are the arches of both feet. These too should be regularly massaged.

Meditation for Capricorn

"I know that my feeling of duty and responsibility is the way that spiritual love expresses through me. I recognize that this is the source of my urge and feeling for these things. And for me this is the highest form of love. My talent for management and organization is an authentic gift from the Most High and it was given for a reason – to be used. I use it with wisdom and with gratitude to the Source from which it came."

A Spiritual View of Aquarius

Something happened to Capricorn along the path of his/her ambitions. Something happened to the soul in its exploration of the past – of the lessons of history, of tradition. For when it goes back far enough it discovers that there were MANY traditions of "doing things" – of reaching the heights. There were – and are – many ways, all of them time-tested to manage things. There were – and are – many possible applications and arrangements of basic truths. Very often the difference between them is strictly a matter of preference and convenience.

Something new has opened up to the soul. It discovers that the MOST ANCIENT can be – and often is – the MOST MODERN, the most AVANT-GARDE, the most RADICAL! New systems – new technology, new social forms, new religions – are generally nothing more than the most ancient with a slightly different twist.

Tradition has liberated the Capricorn from tradition. "The test of time" – the great bugaboo to Capricorn's further progress – has liberated him/her from the "test of time."

The soul is ready to enter the Aquarius experience.

There are many who say that Aquarius is the great iconoclast – the "breaker of traditions." But this is not strictly true. It only seems that way. In reality the Aquarian falls back on an even "older tradition" to break with the present one. He/she uses one tradition to break with another.

Tradition, as we have mentioned earlier, represents the "sum of mankind's solutions for survival." One does not tamper with this lightly. One must actually prove – demonstrate – that the new solution is in fact better, more workable than anything presently available. And this is the task and challenge of Aquarius. In order to change a tradition, something that is long established, one must – almost by definition – have knowledge.

One must KNOW, not guess or surmise, for very often survival depends on it. And thus the Aquarian has an ingrained urge to know. This urge to know gives birth to SCIENCE (as we understand it) and to the rigorous methods of science.

In order to achieve this state that we call "knowing," one must first believe that the universe – nature – is knowable. That it is rational. That it operates by law, and that this law can be discerned and applied by humans. Science is a religion in this sense.

In Aquarius the soul remembers its capacity for omniscience. That within it is already contained all knowledge. And it also recognizes its absolute right and authority to make this knowledge conscious and to use this knowledge to better itself and its fellow humans.

"True and correct knowledge," says Aquarius, "is the great breaker of all binding tradition. It is the great liberator that sets the captives free."

There's a lot of truth there.

Whatever new knowledge the Aquarian gains will eventually become part of a new tradition. At some point, another Aquarian genius will have to "break with that." It's one continuous cycle of establishing and breaking tradition.

The freedom and liberation that Aquarius seems to crave is not some kind of absolute freedom (this will happen in Pisces) but the freedom to create its own "tradition" – its own lifestyle – based on its own theories and perceptions of truth. Once the Aquarius has gained this "freedom" it becomes quite "conservative" in it.

But merely having knowledge is not enough to start a new tradition. The knowledge must be verified scientifically by others. This means that it has to be taught and communicated to others. And this means that observations and laws have to be codified so that others can understand it. And so communication is one of the gifts of Aquarius. The ability of "equals" to work together harmoniously in groups is also one of the important gifts of the Aquarius. For without this, science (which is really a group effort) would be impossible. The power to construct theories and hypotheses from masses of seemingly unrelated facts is another of the gifts of Aquarius.

Generally the cultivation of knowledge doesn't make for good human relationships. Different faculties are required. But Aquarius is different. They cultivate a friendly – but cool – sociability, precisely the kind of relationship that best promotes the exchange of knowledge and information. Clear, friendly, but non-passionate. Slightly aloof. Too much passion interferes with the power to think clearly – and thus the more passionate types are mystified by Aquarius – and the Aquarius is often unfairly characterized as being "cold," "soulless," "unfeeling." However, the Aquarius is much better at human relationship than the Virgo – the other scientist-technologist of the zodiac.

The science of astrology is ruled by Aquarius (and by Uranus, its ruling planet). For all new knowledge – all revelation – comes from the "heavens" the kingdom of mind.

Aquarius excels in all the sciences, in astrology, in the media – especially the electronic media – in art that is avant-garde, as inventors, in political movements of an egalitarian nature, as revolutionaries, in group healing or group therapy, selling to groups, engineering, computers – software or hardware – and fields dealing with the latest technology.

The most favorable periods of the year for Aquarius are January 21 – February 21 (Sun in Aquarius); May 21 – June 21 (Sun in Gemini); September 21 – October 21 (Sun in Libra). Its most favorable days of a given month are when the Moon is in Aquarius, Libra or Gemini (approximately one fourth of the month). Its most favorable day of the week is Saturday. Its most favorable hours of the day are the hours of Saturn (co-ruler of Aquarius) and when Aquarius, Gemini, or Libra is rising. (This is definitely modified by individual factors in the horoscope and by the transits of the planets. But what we're trying to say is that all things being equal these periods will be more favorable than other periods. That is, Moon in Gemini with good aspects will be more favorable for Aquarius than Moon in Scorpio with good aspects – or Moon in Leo with good aspects.)

Aquarius rules the ankles – and by reflex, the wrists. These should be massaged regularly, but especially when the transits are stressed.

The colors of Aquarius are black, gray, and electric or ultramarine blue. Its metals are lead and uranium. Its gems are opals, black pearls and sapphires. Its plants and herbs are gardenia, azalea (co-ruled by Mercury), dragonwort, and spikenard.

Meditation for Aquarius

"I recognize that the universe and everything in it was conceived by an Infinite Thinker that knows itself and its creation perfectly. Everything which transpires is transpiring in this mind – the first and ultimate cause of All. I am ONE with that mind now. Never was I separated from it, except in thought and belief. And since I am one with that mind – that Omniscience within – I partake of this Omniscience in accordance with my ability to receive and accept it. I open wide the gates of my mind to it now and let that Omniscience flow through me – illuminate me – initiate me into all the mysteries of nature, of man, of the universe. Omniscience is clarifying my conscious now. Omniscience is solving my problems now. Omniscience is guiding me now, in the personal and the universal. I am at peace. I know and I know that I know. And presently I shall see this knowing confirmed by my experience."

A Spiritual View of Pisces

For sure, Pisces is one of the "mystery signs" of the zodiac. Very difficult to understand Pisces and, in truth, Pisces likes it that way. Like the ocean there are depths, heights, undercurrents and entire worldlets in the nature. You have to keep this in mind when dealing with Pisces.

If you want to understand Pisces you will have to be patient and do it very gradually. There is too much going on in the nature for them to reveal themselves all at once – even if it were possible. It takes lifetimes to explore and understand even the physical oceans of the planet, let alone the "cosmic ocean of the Universal Consciousness" which Pisces represents. There are worlds within worlds within worlds. Dreams within dreams. Revelations within revelations. Currents and subcurrents.

In my opinion this sign has been misunderstood and even misrepresented by professional astrologers, who presumably should know better. But this is part of the cross that Pisces has to bear and Pisces knows how to deal with it.

In Pisces the soul has undergone all experience. It is really the summation of ALL the powers and faculties of all the other signs – for remember that each sign is a progression of all that went before. Because of this, some astrologers (out of a certain pique, no doubt) have called it "the dustbin of the zodiac." We presume that they mean that it has all the flaws of all the previous signs. Perhaps. But if this true on the "negative side" then it is equally true on the "positive side" – Pisces is also the summation of the highest faculties and powers of the entire zodiac.

In Pisces the soul has scaled the mental heights of Aquarius, has experienced the pinnacles of power and position in Capricorn, has traveled the world in Sagittarius, has known love and rapture in Leo and Libra. What else is left for it? Why does it still feel unhappy and dissatisfied? Has it perhaps omitted something? Is it being punished for some sin? Is there something "wrong" with the soul?

Pisces generally sets itself to find out and learn about it.

In the beginning, the Pisces doesn't yet realize that the vague dissatisfaction that it feels from all the pinnacles that the materialists and worldly-minded crave and exalt is only the "call" – the "signal" of another faculty-power-gift – that wants to unfold and express itself through him/her. It is the "call" of the transcendental part of the nature making itself felt. It is the archangel of the Presence troubling the waters in order to get its attention.

"Come up higher, my beloved, I have something wonderful to show you. Come up higher, I have gifts better than diamonds and gold and name and fame. Come up higher, I have mysteries that cannot be revealed to the profane."

Pisces, more than most, is open to this call. (Remember that we are talking about the Pisces "type" and not necessarily someone who has the Sun in Pisces. A person of any sign with Neptune strong in the nativity – or with many planets in Pisces – would also exhibit this tendency.)

In Aquarius the soul has mastered all knowledge. All that can be known by reason and intellect is known. But the soul still feels that there are many, many more dimensions of knowledge that it cannot access. Its methodology – its approach – is at fault. Certain things cannot be known by ordinary scientific means. The faculty of transcendence is necessary. The power of "union" (or yoga) is necessary. The gift of faith must be acquired. And this the soul explores in Pisces.

In Aquarius the soul "knows." In Pisces the soul "understands."

It's one thing to "know" something – to use it and build with it and achieve with it – but understanding something is different. Understanding has to do with "meaning." One can know all about the atom – its structure and function, etc. One can even know enough about it to create bombs or nuclear reactors but that doesn't mean that one "understands" it. Understanding has to do with understanding its "place, position and significance in the scheme of things" – its right use. If functional power comes from knowledge, then "appreciation" (a bit different from love but related) comes from understanding.

Transcendence is the ability to "rise above" any condition – whether it be material, mental, emotional or historical – and to view it from a cosmic perspective. From this ability come understanding, new knowledge and healing. So important is this urge at times that it will even dominate the urges for food, sex and pleasure. For when properly done it is more rapturous than any of these things. This is the great secret that mystics down through the ages knew and which the soul discovers in Pisces.

There are certain subtle uneases in the soul that only transcendence – the cosmic perspective – can cure. There is no other cure. In Scorpio the soul learned to transcend in order to transform itself and its environment. But in Pisces the soul transcends in order to understand and comprehend. It may or may not decide to change things. Very often the transcendental consciousness reveals that "there is nothing that needs to be changed – everything is perfect, going according to plan." Very often – and this is quite amazing! – the very act of transcendence changes things. It must be experienced to be understood.

Through the faculty of transcendence the soul learns the origins of all "suffering" and also its cure. And thus the Pisces type is very interested in the relief of suffering. In Virgo the soul heals on the physical plane but does not – essentially – touch the cause of disease. In Pisces the healing takes place on deeper levels – at the root and the source of the disease – which is always spiritual in nature, something that the soul has not understood or comprehended about Reality which causes it to form concepts and take actions that obstruct the flow of life force from the Source.

In Virgo, healing and hygiene are personal – one on one. In

Pisces healing is both personal and universal. The Pisces wants to heal the world. In healing one person it knows that the entire world is just that much healthier.

In Aquarius, the knowledge that the soul gains is by scientific methods – observation, experiment, thought, theory, etc. These are powerful tools. But in Pisces – through the faculty of transcendence – the soul gains knowledge by "direct experience" of the thing, or process, or law. This is done by union. For example, if the Aquarius were studying the Moon, he would observe it by telescope, calculate its movements, orbit and phases, observe what happens on Earth when the Moon is in such and such a position, and afterwards would form theories based on these observations. The Pisces would approach the problem differently. He wouldn't negate the exterior observations of the scientist, but he would learn about the Moon by "becoming the Moon." He would reason thus: "The Moon is a created entity in the Great Universal Mind – therefore it is an aspect of consciousness, therefore it has some life and intelligence inherent in it, therefore it is possible for an aspect of my own consciousness to 'unite with it,' to get into 'rapport' with it – and thus learn about it from the 'inside.'" An unorthodox way of getting knowledge to be sure, but most major breakthroughs in knowledge happen that way. For Pisces would approach the Moon with "other faculties" than those with which the scientist would approach it. He or she would approach it from the "inside." He would let the Moon herself describe herself to him. Of course without the transcendental faculty such explorations are impossible.

Thus faith is important to Pisces. But the faith of Pisces is far from "naiveté" (though they are often accused of this by those who can't understand) – it is the recognition that "faith is the bridge to knowledge," that faith holds the "metaphysical universe" together, that faith is the "substance of things hoped for," the "substance of ideas." Without faith it is impossible to transcend and through transcendence the capacity for faith is enlarged.

If the Infinite Mind did not "believe in itself" when it "spoke the universe into existence," or if it doubted its ability to create, or disbelieved in – or denied – its "creation" for even an instant, the universe could not exist.

Indeed faith holds the universe together.

Pisces is always transcending – consciously or unconsciously. When it has not been instructed in the correct ways to do it, it will often resort to drugs, alcohol or sex. These things are attractive to them not so much because of their inherent pleasure, but because it is an easy form of escape from an uncomfortable or untenable emotional, mental or physical condition. But when the Pisces is instructed in the correct procedures it usually lets go of these things.

It is in the exploration of the "invisible side" of things that Pisces finds its greatest fulfillment and success. For here we find the sources of all artistic inspiration, scientific knowledge, and spiritual enlightenment. Capricorn says, "The invisible might exist, but since I can't see it or 'touch it' it might as well – from the 'practical' point of view – not exist. I shall rule over the 'visible' and the knowable." Pisces says, "That's OK but the invisible is more important, more real, more powerful, more causative than the visible. Therefore I shall master the invisible and thus rule the visible indirectly."

Is it any wonder that Pisces is a mystery to friend and foe alike? Is it any wonder that the materialists and the plutocrats cannot understand them? That they seem so elusive and "slippery" to the materialistic mind?

A Pisces who knows how to transcend can escape any net of matter. For he/she operates from another dimension and in another "medium."

Pisces is the natural ruler of the Twelfth House. This house – among other things – is called "the prison house of the personality and the liberation of the soul." This is an interesting contradiction. But very often the faculty of transcendence – which leads to real freedom – is best developed when the "three-dimensional self" is most in "bondage," apparently "cramped," seemingly "unfree." Thus there is motivation – and desperate need – to call on the higher faculties. Until such a state is reached too many will rely on their "three-dimensional faculties" to bail them out.

If you understand that Pisces' main objective is to develop and perfect his/her faculty of transcendence (and not necessarily to be "successful" in the worldly sense) you will understand why this so-called "bondage" or self-undoing attributed to them is far from a tragedy.

Pisces excels in all the arts, but especially in music, poetry, dance, and creative writing. They are natural psychics, metaphysicians, healers, anesthesiologists, correction officers, social workers, podiatrists, reflexologers, parapsychologists, astrologers, prophets, spiritual or occult researchers, seers and mystics.

Industries that deal with these things are good for Pisces. Ships and the shipping industry, the Navy, the fishing industry, the oil industry, the shoe industry, the hosiery industry, pharmaceuticals, charitable institutions, monasteries, film and entertainment are also excellent. Pisces excels in any job where "inspiration" – the faculty of being able to contact more refined states of consciousness – is necessary.

The most favorable periods of the year for Pisces are February 21 – March 21 (Sun in Pisces); June 21 – July 21 (Sun in Cancer); October 21 – November 21 (Sun in Scorpio). The most favorable periods in a given month are when the Moon is in Cancer, Scorpio or Pisces. The most favorable day of the week is Thursday. The most favorable hours of the day are the hours of Jupiter and when Cancer, Scorpio or Pisces is rising. (Individual factors in the horoscope and the daily transits will modify these interpretations – sometimes drastically. But what we mean is that all things being equal, these periods will be more favorable than other periods with equivalent aspects.)

The colors of Pisces are white, deep indigo and deep blue-green (ocean colors). Its metals are tin and platinum. Its gems are peridot, chrysolite, moonstone, and coral. Its scents are lotus, opium and coffee. Its plants and herbs are opium, tobacco, mimosa, coffee, seaweed, lotus, sea moss, and plants that grow beneath the sea.

Pisces rules the feet and these should be regularly massaged, but especially when the transits are stressful. This is a healthy practice for anybody as the feet contain the reflexes to the entire body, but it is especially healthful for Pisces.

Meditation for Pisces

"I am an immortal being of light, one with God and in perfect union and harmony with the universe. This is not some future condition, nor is it something that I create. It is so now. The actual state of affairs. One with this wisdom, I am guided constantly on the path I shall follow. One with this wisdom, I am a channel through which it flows into the world. One with this wisdom, there is no confusion or wavering in my mind. I am wherever I choose to be. I am doing what I love to do, being where I love to be, among the people that I love to be with. I am in absolute harmony, fulfilling my destiny."

Some Perspectives on the Houses

The signs of the zodiac represent twelve attitudes to life, twelve powers of the soul, twelve spiritual faculties and abilities. The twelve houses represent twelve sectors of experience, twelve areas of interest, twelve different scenes of action, twelve priorities of importance to the native. Though the signs and the houses are related and similar, they are NOT the same thing.

For example, the fact that someone has the Sun in Aries does not give us the complete picture of the native. If that Aries' Sun is in the First House it will mean one thing; if it occurs in the Second House it will mean something else and so forth and so on for each house.

When we analyze a person's "signs of power" – the signs that contain the most planets – we are looking at the strength of certain faculties, abilities and personalities in the native's psyche. But when we analyze a person's "houses of power" we are looking at the areas of life that the native finds most interesting – the areas of life that are "priorities" to the native.

Thus, regardless of whether a native is an Aries or Taurus or Gemini or whatever, if there is power in the Second House (i.e. many planets there, or if the Sun or Moon is there) there will be a tremendous interest in "making money," acquiring possessions, etc.

If a person has power in Taurus or Capricorn which gives "materialistic ability" AND there is power in the Second House we know that the person's interest in money and things – his/her earning abilities – are accentuated. One power is reinforcing the other.

Knowing a person's "natural interests and hobbies" is important for BOTH the astrologer and the client to understand. Very often the astrologer sees areas of interest that are not "being fed" by the client – not being pursued – often causing some feelings of "dissatisfaction," frustration, etc. Also a house analysis enables us to see the native's attitude and aptitude in every major area of life, which tells us what kind of person he/she is and how he/she is likely to behave in different areas.

House analysis is also very important in compatibility analysis (synastry). For one of the factors that "keep people together" (aside from the natural chemistry between them) are the areas of common interest. No matter what the "spiritual chemistry" is between two people, mutual power in the same houses could bring them together. For example, let's assume two people with a terrible natural chemistry between them. If they both had power in the Second House they would have a common interest in money making and this common interest would tend to be a bond between them – a shaky one, but a bond nevertheless.

If the natural chemistry between two people is basically good AND we also find many of the same houses of power in each chart, the bond between these two people will be much stronger than if there were no common interests.

House analysis gives us a whole new dimension in horoscope interpretation.

We define a "House of Power" as any house that has two or more planets in it. One planet in a house denotes an interest, but not a dominant interest. Two or more show a strong interest. The only exception is if the house contains one of the big three – the Sun, the Moon or the Lord of the Ascendant. These planets are so powerful that even the presence of one of them makes a house a House of Power.

If the First House is a house of power in your horoscope you tend to be very interested in your physical body, its care and maintenance, personal appearance and the self-image that you project. You care very deeply about how other people see you and how you see yourself. Your image is very important to you. Your self-esteem, self-confidence are very important to you. You give these areas a lot of attention. You excel in fields that deal with developing self-image, self-esteem, etc. You KNOW that these things are NOT really you, but you are very aware of the power your own personal image has on others and thus on your happiness.

If the ruler and the planets in the First House are well aspected (by birth or by transit), you would tend to have a healthy and desirable self-image. You would tend to be very expert in this area.

If the ruler (the causative principle or ruling genius) and the occupants of the First House have stressful aspects (by birth or by transit) there would tend to be problems in creating, forming and/or manifesting the desired self-image and there would undoubtedly be strong feelings of "self-denial" – lack of self-worth and lack of self-confidence.

Since so much of life is based on "perception" and not deep truth this is indeed an important house. All too often we are judged by how we "appear" and not on who we really are.

Too much power in this house could make one "vain" – too concerned about appearances, too concerned about image rather than substance and reality.

The ideal, of course, is a "good person" in a "pleasing package." And we should work towards that – ignoring neither one nor the other.

If the Second House is a house of power in your horoscope you would be very interested in making money, acquiring wealth, acquiring material things. Your personal earning power is very important to you and you tend to give it most of your attention and thought. If the Sun or the ascendant ruler is also in the Second House, your whole sense of ego and self-esteem could be tied up with your earning power to a point where when income goes down, so does self-esteem and self-confidence – even when the loss or drop in income is no fault of your own. People with a lot of power in the Second House generally attain wealth. If the aspects to the ruler and the occupants are easy (by birth and by transit), wealth will be attained rather easily. If the aspects to the ruler or the occupants are stressful, wealth tends to come through difficulties and the overcoming of many, many obstacles – sometimes it is delayed, sometimes the native never feels satisfied no matter how much he/she has. Second House types are basically interested in "making money" and not so much in "prestige" or power – unless there is strong power in the Tenth House.

They are "bottom line" types – not overly concerned about "how" they make it or whether their means of acquisition are socially prestigious or not.

If the Third House is a house of power in your horoscope, communication is very important to you. Relations with brothers and sisters are very important to you, as are relations with your neighbors. You excel in the media and as a writer, journalist, advertising or public relations person. Marketing, sales, teaching, lecturing are also good fields for you and you have a strong interest in all these things. You are a reader as well as a writer. Self-expression, in logical and intellectual ways, is one of your fundamental drives and needs.

If the ruler and the occupying planets are well aspected (by birth or by transit) you are probably considered "gifted" in these areas. Relations with brothers, sisters, and neighbors are – probably – harmonious.

If these planets are stressed (by birth or by transit) you are probably experiencing difficulties and problems in these areas – very frustrating to you precisely because you consider them to be so important.

If the Fourth House is a house of power in your horoscope (regardless of what your Sun sign may be) the home and the family is a major interest in your life. Family values in general are very important to you. You tend to spend more energy and attention on these areas than other people would. You are perhaps overly concerned about your physical and emotional environment raising the family – nurturing them. You are a "nest builder."

You excel in industries that deal with residential real-estate, cooking, maternity. You also excel in professions where you can "work from the home."

If the ruler and the occupying planets are well aspected (by birth or by transit) your home and domestic life tends to be harmonious, fulfilling and satisfying.

If these planets are stressed (by birth or by transit) you are undoubtedly experiencing difficulties in your domestic situation and interests.

If the Fifth House is a house of power in your horoscope, you are a "fun-lover." You are interested in the things that "add rapture" to life. Creativity, entertainment, going out, parties, love affairs, gambling and speculating are very important to you. Life is not worth living unless you're having a good time. Children are very important to you, as many consider this to be the "ultimate in creativity." You like to bring pleasure to others as well as yourself, for when others are having a good time it increases your own "rapture."

You tend to excel at (or appreciate) music, drama, film, and art. If the ruler and the occupying planets are well aspected (easy by birth or by transit) you DO tend to have a good time in life. You tend to be a "lucky speculator" and have pleasure from your children.

If the ruler and the occupying planets are stressed (by birth or by transit) you are probably having difficulties with all the affairs of this house. Children might be upsetting you or speculations don't pan out, etc., etc.

If the Sixth House is a house of power in your horoscope you are very concerned with health matters, diet, exercise, keeping fit. Conditions at your place of work are important to you as well as relations with employees and/or fellow workers. You have a strong work ethic and have a need to be useful and productive. You can be a workaholic if you're not careful. You like to do things "right" as a matter of principle and not so much because of money or prestige.

You tend to excel in the medical or nursing professions as well as the whole health industry. If the ruler and the occupying planets are well aspected (by birth or by transit) health and health matters tend to go smoothly – much still depends on other factors in the horoscope. Events at the workplace tend to be harmonious. The native tends to enjoy his work.

If the ruler and the occupying planets are stressed (by birth or by transit) there tends to be problems in all these matters.

If the Seventh House is a house of power in your horoscope your relations with others and your social life are very important to you – a major priority in life. Partnerships are important. And you tend to spend a lot of time and energy on these things. You bend over backwards to please others and are often forced to adapt to situations not of your making.

You tend to excel in social matters and in industries that deal with catering to parties, fine art, matchmaking, diplomacy, etc. (Other factors in the chart could modify this a great deal.)

If the ruler and the occupying planets are well aspected (by birth or by transit), social matters and partnerships tend to be fulfilling, harmonious and satisfying. If the ruler and the occupying planets are stressed (by birth or by transit) the social life tends to be unsatisfying, needing a lot of work to correct.

If the Eighth House is a house of power in your horoscope you tend to be involved in making money for other people – for partners, investors, shareholders, etc. You are concerned with managing other people's money. There is a great interest in death, sex and transformation. You are interested in sex in its power aspect more than its pleasure aspect. You are interested in how to bring about radical changes in your environment, personal condition or corporation. You are the person "who turns things around" either at work or in your personal life.

Occultism and occult power is also a major interest. Death has touched your life early and is something that you need to understand and grapple with.

If the ruler and occupying planets are well aspected (by birth or by transit) you tend to be successful in all these matters.

If the ruler and occupying planets are stressed (by birth or by transit) these matters are causing difficulties – all the more frustrating since they are so important to you. Others might also have problems in these areas – how many people REALLY understand sex and death? – but since it is not such a priority in their lives it is less of a problem.

If the Ninth House is a house of power in your horoscope, you are interested in metaphysics, philosophy, religion and higher education in general. You like to travel to foreign countries. You tend to excel in all these industries.

If the ruler and occupying planets are well aspected (by birth or by transit) these affairs tend to go smoothly.

If the ruler and occupying planets are stressed (by birth or by transit) these matters tend to be "difficult."

If the Tenth House is a house of power in your horoscope, you are very ambitious in a worldly sense. You long for the "peaks." Your social status and position in the world are VERY important to you. Your public image – your public prestige – takes up a lot of your time and thought. Tenth House types sometimes think that this is all that life is about – the attainment of status. Money is important to you but HOW you earn it is more important to you. Very often you will forego positions that pay more in favor of positions that are more socially prestigious. Fame, recognition, honor are important goals.

If the ruler and the occupying planets are well aspected (by birth or by transit) you tend to attain to these things pretty harmoniously and naturally.

If the ruler and the occupying planets are stressed (by birth or by transit) it is much more difficult to attain to these things though you try with all your might.

If the Eleventh House is a house of power in your horoscope, friendships and working with groups are very important to you. You like to communicate and teach – but on a big scale through the mass media. You are interested in science and humanitarian groups.

If the ruler and occupying planets are well aspected (by birth or by transit) you tend to enjoy harmonious friendships and the other matters of this house tend to be expressed harmoniously. If the ruler and occupying planets are stressed (by birth or by transit) you tend to have problems with friends and with the other matters of this house.

If the Twelfth House is a house of power in your horoscope, you enjoy seclusion, mystical and religious studies, charitable works, psychic phenomena and dreams. You like to avoid the "public eye" and lead a more "subjective type" of existence. You long to explore the inner kingdoms of your mind. You need to enter careers that allow you this kind of freedom.

If the ruler and occupying planets are well aspected (by birth or by transit) you tend to enjoy great success in these matters. If the ruler and occupying planets are stressed (by birth or by transit) there is difficulty in these matters – the urge for seclusion can mean prison or a hospital ward; psychic science can become deception of the self and others.

Minutes of a Symposium on the Meaning of Life

In the great University of Atma which is located in the country called Abstract in the Fortress called Within, a symposium took place recently. It was an open meeting. The souls of all men and women of Earth were in attendance, though many of them were asleep to the proceedings.

Also in attendance were the souls of the most illustrious illuminati that ever walked the Earth. There is not space here to list all of them by name. Suffice it to say that beings of the stature and magnitude of Plato, Pythagoras, Zarathrustra, Moses, Jesus, Buddha, Mohammed, Christian Rosenkreuz, along with many, many of their disciples and companions – each a genuine saint, adept, master in his or her own right – were present.

Great was the energy in the auditorium.

It seemed to me that we were in the upper regions of Briah – the regions where it begins to merge with Origination.

The Ancient of Days began the meeting by invoking the Twelve Lords of Life. They appeared instantly, forming a circle around him.

"We are gathered here to gain a deeper understanding of Life. Who better to discuss this with than the twelve gatekeepers through which it flows? My question to the panel is this: what is the meaning of life? Let us begin in the East and proceed sequentially."

Aries

[He is a tall, young, muscular man with red hair. He wears a ram's headdress studded with rubies and garnets. He carries a shield and a spear and looks ready for a fight. He is naked from the waist up. Behind him are hordes of armed men.]

"Life is the development of courage. For without courage the soul cannot cross the abyss to Divinity. Without courage the soul cannot overcome inertia, cannot act with power in its sphere. Without courage the soul is enslaved to alien forces. Without courage it cannot progress. Without courage new frontiers of good are forever sealed off. What better way to develop courage than by leading a life of risk and adventure! That which it most fears, that should the soul do. I love the very center of danger though I perish, for there I learn courage. There is no greater achievement than the conquest of fear."

Taurus

[A beautiful but heavy-set woman – stocky – with a thick strong neck; a winged bull sits beside her. She is fully clothed in robes of earth tones studded with emeralds. Her eyes are green. Behind her are vast farms where cattle graze and giant cows are being milked.]

"Life is the development of a sense of ease. For without ease the soul cannot progress to its divine estate. And without substance, the wherewithal of life, activity and progress are impossible. Without substance the soul is not at ease and cannot think about higher things. Without substance the soul cannot progress on its path of perfection. To lack substance is to lack ease. To lack ease is to lack health. To lack health is to lack life and power. The soul must cross the abyss to Divinity in wealth and comfort. If there is any unease in the crossing the unease will pull it down. One should approach Divinity with perfect gifts, for Divinity will not accept gifts that are imperfect."

Gemini

[A young boy and a young girl – identical twins. Both are naked. Tall and slim. There are wings on their feet. It is the boy who speaks.]

"Life is the orderly manifestation of the Word. Word by word the soul creates its circumstances. Word by word doth it ascend or descend in vibration. The better the word, the better the circumstances the soul can abide in. Without the word there is no ease, no creation, no universe. I live for the word and by the word. By means of the word doth the soul bind itself to its ineffable Source. By the word is the soul saved."

Cancer

[A beautiful but mature woman in silver robes. She is holding a child close to an exposed breast from which it is suckling. Behind her is a vast blue-green ocean.]

"Family and motherhood is the highest aim of life. Without motherhood nothing gets born. And without family nothing survives. A mother's love is the closest the soul comes to divine, unconditional love in the world of mortals. I live to be mother. I long to be mother."

Leo

[A strong, muscular, blond-haired man at the prime of his strength. He wears a golden crown and holds a golden scepter in his right hand. Two golden lions are on either side.]

"Rapture is the only true meaning of life. Life is meaningless without joy. Where life really is, there is joy. Without joy there is only pseudo life – a mere shadow of what life should be. Rapture under will is the law. With rapture do I execute my will and my will is rapture. Without rapture the soul is too heavy and earthbound to cross the abyss. Rapture brings the soul unto the Most High."

Virgo

[A beautiful young brown-haired woman – stunning in her perfection. Her eyes face downward demurely. She holds a stalk of wheat in her hands and behind her are vast wheat fields.]

"Service to others is the ultimate and highest meaning of life. Service is love in action. In service love fulfills itself. Without service the plan of the Most High could never manifest. Joy lifts the soul unto the divine, but service brings the divine to Earth."

Libra

[A lovely lady in a sheer green negligee. Her buttocks and hips are completely exposed and perfectly formed. She holds a mirror in her left hand and scales in her right. Her hair is golden and she wears a wreath of red roses.]

"Love and beauty are the ultimate aims of life. Love is the supreme motivating power in heaven and Earth and without love no soul ascendeth unto the Father. Beauty is the ultimate truth. Beauty is the guide to all aspiring souls. He who knoweth not beauty knoweth not the Most High."

Scorpio

[A proud, haughty man, perfectly formed. Beside him is a beautiful black lady. He has a firm grip on her as if to keep her there by force. Behind them is a tunnel leading to the deeps of the Earth. The lady speaks.]

"The meaning of life is sex and death. Death is a form of sex and sex a form of death. Only through continuous disintegration doth new life manifest. Unless the mortal dieth it cannot be born again. And unless he is 'born again' he cannot enter the precincts of life eternal. I live to die. I die to live. There is nothing greater than death. Death is the ultimate power. Death is the ultimate good. Death is the ultimate liberator. The seed dieth in order to become a plant. The egg dieth in order to become a chick. The mortal dieth in order to become immortal. Death is the ultimate sexual act – the ultimate creative action – the ultimate passion. Continuous death is the secret of life eternal. Happy are those who know how to die."

Sagittarius

[A large and powerful paternal figure, sitting on a throne on top of a high mountain. He holds a scepter in one hand and a lightning bolt in the other. His position is high above the audience. His consort is beside him. He descends to the auditorium in order to speak. His consort remains on the mountain top. The smell of jasmine and myrrh permeates the hall. Lightning bolts flash from his head every time he speaks and these bolts enter the minds of selected people in the audience who seem to enjoy it.]

"The meaning of life is the acquisition of wisdom. There is nothing greater than this. Wisdom is intelligence motivated by love. Without wisdom love is a shallow personal force; the cause more often of war and inharmony than good. Love needs wisdom to discern the highest good. Wisdom alone exalts and elevates love and makes of it something Divine. Without wisdom there is no discernment of the divine plan, and mortals soon lose their way. Wisdom knows all about love and sex and death and life. In wisdom we discern the meaning of life, whence we come and where we shall go. Happy are they who love wisdom and who practice it. Happy are they who travel far and wide in search of it. Happy are they who allow themselves to be guided by it. Healthy are they who allow themselves to be mastered by it."

Capricorn

[A very old man, dressed in black and indigo robes. His consort is a very large elderly woman. He holds a scythe in one hand and a clock in the other. She holds a cornucopia on her lap and there is a winged goat beside her. The lady speaks.]

"There is nothing higher than duty. Doing one's allotted task in time and on time is the ultimate meaning and beauty of life. For unless the soul fulfilleth its duty to life, each according to its status and understanding, it cannot progress but must ever return until its duty is fulfilled. Love is mere sensual emotion – the least little hurt or pang and the lover is soon a hater. Duty alone transcends emotion. A soul that loves, truly and wisely, will always do its duty. The ultimate meaning in life is the soul's quest for its divinely assigned duty and then the doing of it. For did not the soul incarnate in order to manifest some aspect of the plan? To concretize its segment of Divinity? Shall it allow sensuous emotion to interfere with that?"

Aquarius

[A paternal figure who looks as if the sky had crystallized into man. He is in light-blue robes with the clearest blue eyes imaginable. He has a son who is similarly dressed and who is carrying a large jug of water. The son speaks.]

"Knowledge is the ultimate meaning and purpose in life. There is nothing greater than true and correct knowledge. The faculty of knowing is man's ultimate salvation. Without true and correct knowledge – which comes from long experience but which is ever new and fresh – one cannot cross the abyss to Divinity. Knowledge is power. Without knowledge the soul cannot fulfill its duty and function to life. Without knowledge man cannot evolve and progress is arrested. By knowledge man fell and by knowledge he shall be redeemed."

Pisces

[A great sea king and sea queen facing in opposite directions. He holds a trident in one hand and a net in the other. She holds a golden cup. The sea queen speaks.]

"Faith and transcendence are the ultimate powers and purposes of life. Transcendence heals all things, dissolves all that should be dissolved and reveals all things. By the power of transcendence do we reach our ultimate unity. And by faith do we transcend and by faith do we live and by faith do we erect the bridges to new knowledge. The soul who hath knowledge of transcendence is forever free – none can obstruct it, none can enslave it, none can hurt it. By faith do we transcend and by transcendence do we acquire the gift of faith."

And then the Ancient of Days spoke

"Indeed ye are all correct though you seem to contradict and clash. For ye are all part of a larger whole. And at different times and different stages each of you take priority. This is the plan of creation. The dance of life. We will now adjourn this meeting. Our next symposium will deal with questions from our audience."

This reporter – being only a journalist and not a participant – does not make any pretense to knowing whether the words uttered at this symposium are true or untrue. This was not his function. His job was merely to report the proceedings and let those for whom this document was intended decide these issues for themselves.

The fact that you are in possession of this document means that you are indeed qualified to discern these issues.

Minutes of a Second Symposium on the Meaning of Life

The symposium on the meaning of life reconvened the next evening. The Ancient of Days again called the meeting to order and again invoked the Twelve Lords of the Life Power. Once again they appeared instantaneously in a circle around him.

"Now," said the Ancient of Days, "we will take questions from the audience."

A woman – the soul of a well-known saint here on Earth – arose. "Speak to us about love. For on the Earth there is no subject more confusing to us. What is love?"

"Let the discussion begin from the East and continue sequentially," said the Ancient of Days.

Aries

"Love is the faculty of being who you are – true to thyself and accepting others for who they are – and not trying to change their essence."

Taurus

"Love is having and holding the beloved and to be had and held by him. Each is the blissful captive of the other. Blessed be the ties that bind."

Gemini

"Love is the right word rightly spoken at the right time. Without this there can be no love."

Cancer

"Words are not love and love is not of the intellect. The feeling of love is love. So long as I feel loved I am loved."

Leo

"Love is rapturing the beloved. Giving the beloved the fullness of joy and pleasure. Love is the bringing of bliss to another."

Virgo

"Love is service above self. Serving the other as you would yourself be served."

Libra

"Love is harmony and justice. Perfect love is perfect fairness and this produces perfect harmony."

Scorpio

"Love is the willingness to make war – and to die if need be – for the beloved. But even more than this, it is the willingness to die to oneself to self-transform – in the interest of the beloved."

Sagittarius

"Love is wisdom's consort. One must love under wisdom so that one can discern the true need of the beloved and fulfill it. Without wisdom the true need cannot be discerned. And without wisdom there is no power to fulfill."

Capricorn

"Love is one's highest duty to the beloved, and one's highest duty is love. Everything else is mere sentiment and sensuous emotion."

Aquarius

"Love is a total knowing of the beloved – on all levels. Where there is complete knowledge, there is love and love will lead to complete knowledge. How can one love without knowledge? How can one know without love?"

Pisces

"Love is spiritual and divine. It is unconditional and is not in need of any specific object. Love is an Impersonal force that flows from the Most High upon all – the beautiful and the ugly, the saint and the sinner, the noble and the ignoble – equally. Thus should we love."

The Ancient of Days spoke

"Once again you are all correct though you seem to contradict. Love is all of this and more. For different souls need different types of loving. And every soul needs different loving at different stages and times. And every soul expresses love in different ways at different times. So it is fitting that there be so many varied meanings and expressions of love.

"Blessed is the ONE in the MANY. Blessed is the ONE through the MANY."

An Astrological Guide to Aromas

Like most of the New Age arts and sciences, aroma therapy is actually thousands of years old. It is only a rediscovery by us moderns of pieces of an ancient wisdom.

There are many ways that aromas are used therapeutically. They can be used in massage, in baths and in ointments to ease a specific condition or to promote a general sense of well-being.

They can be used to create a mood – an atmosphere – in your environment, for fun or for therapy.

I have found them to be especially dramatic in meditation and spiritual practice – which was one of the major ways they were used in ancient times.

In meditation the idea is to think along a predetermined set of thoughts consciously willed by the operator. These thought patterns can vary depending on the object of the meditation. There is no question that certain aromas facilitate certain thoughts and feelings. Much easier to think thoughts of love and harmony with aromas ruled by Venus than with aromas ruled by other planets. Much easier to elevate the mind, to enter a state of worship and reverence with aromas ruled by Jupiter and Neptune than with other aromas. With all the distractions of everyday life – most of which are operating contrary to these states – we need all the help we can get.

This power to facilitate thought/mood/feeling is something that each of you can experience for yourselves. Aromas, since they appeal to a different sense, can be effectively used with light, color, and sound to amplify and strengthen any mood or state that we desire to create.

One simple way to use aromas – and this is not the only way – is to wear the scent of your Sun sign. Since the Sun in your chart represents the real you – the immortal part of you – wearing the appropriate scent would remind you of who you really are. It would help you to maintain a stronger contact – conscious contact – with that aspect of yourself, the solar being within. You would be more responsive to its guidance and protection – more open to its genius. And this, after all, is the object of life.

This is also the rationale for wearing the gemstones and colors of your Sun sign. For, as we have mentioned elsewhere, there is nothing "higher" in life than being yourself.

Here are the scents for the different signs.

(Sources for these rulerships are *The Rulership Book* by Rex Bills, *A Garden of Pomegranates* by Israel Regardie and Culpepper's *Complete Herbal*. In cases where there was conflict between the authorities, the pendulum was used to determine the rulership.)

Aries

Honeysuckle, ginger, civet, peppermint (also co-ruled by the Sun and Leo).

Taurus

Bitter almond, lavender, rose, geranium (or rose geranium as it is listed in some catalogues), tuberose, ylang-ylang, strawberry (co-ruled by Jupiter), clove (co-ruled by Jupiter).

Gemini

Storax (or styrax as it is listed in some catalogues), lilac, lily of the valley.

Cancer

Sandalwood (co-ruled by Pluto), jasmine (co-ruled by Jupiter), wintergreen (co-ruled by Saturn), cucumber.

Leo

Musk, heliotrope, orange or orange blossom, lemon, bergamot

(some say that Pisces is the ruler but my pendulum says it is Leo), frankincense, eucalyptus, chamomile, peppermint, grapefruit.

Virgo
Narcissus, lilac, lily of the valley, storax (or styrax).

Libra
Bitter almond, clove, lavender, rose, geranium, rose geranium, tuberose, ylang-ylang, arnica, apple blossom.

Scorpio
Coconut, cherry blossom, watermelon, sandalwood, ambergris (co-ruled by Neptune).

Sagittarius
Myrrh, jasmine, strawberry, clove, carnation, cedar.

Capricorn
Sweet pea, pine, fir, camphor, wintergreen.

Aquarius
Gardenia, azalea.

Pisces
Lotus, mimosa, hyacinth, ambergris.

These oils can be applied directly to the skin (but in very small amounts as they are pure and undiluted and too much could cause some irritation) or they can be used in various types of aromatizers to cover rooms or they can be added to a handkerchief and thrown into the dryer when you dry your clothes – this will put the scent right into your clothing.

There are many other ways to creatively use these scents. For example, if you were engaged in sales work, or mundane intellectual activity – bookkeeping, letter writing, etc. – you could use the oils of Gemini or Virgo (ruled by Mercury). If you wanted to pray or meditate you could use the oils of Sagittarius and Pisces (ruled by Jupiter and Neptune). If you were throwing a party you could use the oils of Taurus and Libra (ruled by Venus).

It is also possible to create your own scents for money, love or health. Use the Sun sign scent in combination with the scent of the ruler of your Second House and you have a wealth scent. Such a scent would undoubtedly promote wealth ideas in the consciousness. Use a combination of your Sun sign scent with the scent of the ruler of your Seventh or Fifth House (depending on whether you wanted fun or real romance) for love. Such a scent would promote thoughts of love and romance in the consciousness. This is a big field with lots of room for experimentation.

If you would like to learn more about the subject we refer you to *The Art of Aromatherapy* by Robert B. Tisserand; *The Magic of Herbs* by David Conway; *The Rulership Book* by Rex Bills.

The Twelve Yogas

The twelve signs of the zodiac represent twelve aspects of the One Power we call God, Life, the Supreme, the Ineffable. They are the twelve primary ways in which It functions, the twelve different perspectives on life and events, the twelve powers that make the universe go.

But these twelve signs are not only divine functions; they also represent twelve gates to the Divine, twelve portals, twelve ways to connect up to it. Because there are twelve ways – and each is as valid as any of the others – there can be spiritual conflict and misunderstanding among followers of different paths.

Many conflicts in life come from believing that there is only ONE correct "perspective" on things, or only one correct psychological type. Just as family harmony can be enhanced when all the members of the family understand the others' "psychological orientation," so too can many religious schisms be healed by understanding the different paths to the Godhead.

Astrology is an important tool here.

In general, the Fire signs (or people strong in the element of Fire) will gravitate to agni yoga, the yoga of Fire – the primal principle of the universe – and to karma yoga, the yoga of action. Air signs (or people strong in Air signs) will gravitate to jnana yoga, the yoga of the mind, and to prana yoga, the yoga of the universal energy in the air. Water signs (and those very strong in Water) are natural bhakti yogis – they gravitate and excel at the yoga of love and devotion. Earth signs (and those strong in this element) are hatha yogis and get good results from ritual.

Ritual is excellent for Earth types in that it engages the body and uses "concrete" material symbols in the workings. Earth types relate well to this.

It is also important to note that it is rare for any one person to be a "pure type." Most people are combinations of the different types and might feel pulled to a few of these yogas – this would be natural order.

The Yoga of Aries

Since the Aries is built for action, meditative techniques that force one to sit motionless for many hours are not for them. They will be restless and chafe under this kind of discipline. And though many Aries natives are intellectual, too much reading of books or studying of scripture is also not for them. Much better to steer them to a yoga that is aligned with their psychology. Karma yoga – the yoga of pure and disinterested action – right in the world, in daily affairs, is just right. This yoga requires that one "do right" – come from the Divine Will in all one's actions – strictly because it IS right. The result of the action is immaterial – the important thing is the purity of the action. The ultimate result of this yoga will be something akin to what Jesus said: "The Father worketh hitherto and I work." In other words "My actions are not my own, but come from HIM who sent me into expression." I Am God in Action.

In Judaism the practice of doing "mitzvahs" (good deeds) is central to practitioners. The idea is to serve God in the body and in the world and not just abstractly or intellectually. This is a form of karma yoga. Doing mitzvahs can often seem inconvenient or even expensive. Sometimes it leads one into conflict with one's economic or social interest – yet one does them. For a greater reward awaits the person.

But the doing of mitzvahs is just the beginning stages of karma yoga. In the ultimate stages the doer is gone and only the One Doer remains. When this happens there is no need to worry about results as the results will inevitably be good – what else can they be? There could be no negative karma from such actions.

The Yoga of Taurus

Taurus rules the throat and is connected with sound. Thus it stands to reason that, more than most, it would excel in mantra yoga. Sound as a pathway to the Divine. Chanting correct mantras is a very powerful tool. It re-chemicalizes the whole body and transforms it from a mortal body to an immortal one. Mantra invokes spiritual forces into the aura. It cleanses the obstructions to God-realization by uprooting the false patterns of thought and feeling in the psyche. It can heal, enrich and lead one to God Union. Ultimately, the chanter of the mantra will disappear and only the ONE sound, uttered from the One throat, will remain.

Taurus likes "physical and tangible" things. Meditation on "abstract concepts" or invisible forces is not for them. They would get better results from ritual-type prayer – such as Mass, or theurgic rites – than from abstract contemplation.

Hatha yoga which involves physical movement and a physical focus is also suitable for Taurus.

Finally we come to a yoga with no name. Let us call it the yoga of Taurus. Taurus is well known for its love of wealth, material things and material comforts. This is not crass materialism or a sign of superficiality as many claim but just the opposite. It comes from a soul remembrance of the glorious EASE of the living Spirit; that Spirit is always comfortable, always at home, never struggling and always has everything it needs. Taurus is consciously, or unconsciously, working to bring that through. A prolonged meditation on the EASE of God will bring Taurus right to the throne of the Most High. In the beginning there will be many hurdles, as on the human level ease is confused with laziness and selfishness. But the Divine ease is something different. It is ease in action and at rest. The most impossible things (humanly) are easy to the Most High. Mighty works of power are achieved stress-free. Just as there is a yoga of Fire (agni yoga), there is a yoga of Earth – though I have no name to give it. For Earth is as much a spiritual principle as Fire (though it is an end product, where Fire is a First Cause). Thus the yoga of Earth – seeing the divinity and sacredness of this principle – is a valid path for Taurus.

The Yoga of Gemini

The yoga of Gemini is perhaps the most difficult of all the yogas. For it involves a God Union with the intellect and mind. Much easier to attain God Union with other faculties like the feelings than with the mind and intellect.

The feelings are by nature "unitive" and the faculty of faith (so necessary for this project) is more natural. The intellect, on the other hand, is more separative, and faith doesn't come easily to it.

Gemini, like the other Air signs, is comfortable with the jnana yoga approach. They benefit from the study of scripture and sacred writings. They grow from hearing sermons and lectures by spiritual masters. They need spiritual paths that don't offend the intellect, that are rational and logical. The study of Hermetics and occultism is a valid doorway. For these paths show the operations of the Divine Mind in the creation of the universe, man and circumstances. The universe is mind in essence and created by mind. It is logical once the axioms are understood. God created the world using letters, words and numbers – ah, this is something a Gemini can sink his or her teeth into. It is this Divine logic that Gemini is most qualified to penetrate. As their union grows in power it will no longer be the native that thinks, but the One Self that thinks through the native.

Gemini will also benefit greatly from prana yoga and all the various breathing exercises associated with it. Contrary to much of the literature, union with the Divine doesn't mean the "end of all thinking." It only means the end of "mortal thinking." When one is in the Divine Union a whole new set of thoughts come in – thoughts that are congruent to the new state.

The Yoga of Cancer

Cancer, being a Water sign, is a natural bhakti yogi. It is not enough for them to know God or intellectualize about Him – Cancer, like Scorpio and Pisces, wants to feel the presence. So the approach to the Divinity is through the feelings. But the feeling nature of the mortal (like its intellectual nature) is filled with millions of years of impurities. So the Cancerien has a big job on its hands. It will have to sift through feeling by feeling, state by state, emotion by emotion – a mass of psychic detritus. Eventually, their efforts will lead to the "adoration of the Divine Mother" – a shortcut to attainment. Cancer, more than most signs, can succeed at this yoga. For all their natural instincts, when properly understood, are coming from this source – the one, nurturing power of the universe. The One who gave birth to the universe and to all the gods.

Eventually, the Cancerien will become the Divine Mother in incarnation – its true and highest destiny. Male Canceriens need not worry that this path will make them less masculine. If they are male, the Divine Mother will make them even more so – and more correctly so. Further, they will find the Divine Father through the Mother. She will guide them unerringly there. For this is their ultimate destiny.

The Yoga of Leo

Like the Aries, Leo will have a natural affinity with agni yoga, the yoga of Fire – the primal principle of the universe. But along with this they will also have success with the solar yogas – surya yoga (the yoga of the Sun), Krishna yoga and Christ yoga. Meditation on the solar deities of any religion will bring Leo to the Godhead.

The solar yoga (under whatever name we give it) is said to be the most balanced of all the yogas. It includes jnana, agni, bhakti and karma yoga within it. It is an integral yoga – a yoga that allows (actually urges) work in the material world but at the same time without being under the laws of the material world. It blends creativity, outer action, devotion, love and wisdom into one harmonious path.

Many Leos will naturally gravitate to solar type religions, such as Christianity or Buddhism. But this is only a preliminary to the true solar yoga mentioned above.

The Leo, more than most, will be able to find the "Christ Child" within – the playful, innocent divinity that stands above religion and dogma but which is really the object of all religion. This child always "holds the hand" of the Father, and leads the way to it.

The Yoga of Virgo

As with Taurus, the Virgo will excel in the yoga of Earth. This is the yoga that sees the Divine in matter, in all its glory and perfection. THIS world is the kingdom of heaven when rightly understood. In the beginning stages the Virgo will try to "perfect" the world – make it into its own image of perfection. For Virgo knows that the world was perfectly designed and perfectly created. So it will try, by its own efforts, to create this perfection. But as Virgo proceeds into the yoga, it will learn that the world needs no personal perfecting. It is already perfect.

Curiously, once it reaches this realization, the realization itself creates a perfection that couldn't be achieved by personal effort. Its personal efforts cease being personal efforts, but only "follow-throughs" of the Divine Perfection.

The path of humility and self-abnegation is also a valid path for Virgo – and it complements the yoga of Earth mentioned above. But the humility that we speak of is not a human, quasi-hypocritical type of humility. It means that the human person-ality becomes small, so that God can become great. Take away the human ego and personality and what is left? Only God.

Jnana yoga and karma yoga are also valid paths for Virgo. For Virgo is a mental sign, with its mind directed towards the practical affairs of life.

The Yoga of Libra

Libra, being an Air sign, will have a special affinity with jnana yoga, the yoga of mind. It will also get exceptional results from prana yoga and breathing exercises. But its highest form of yoga comes with the contemplation of beauty. Is there such a thing as a yoga of beauty? Perhaps not in standardized form, but it is the path of the artist, poet and musician. At first the Libra will contemplate beauty in its sensual aspects – color, sound, and form. As the contemplation progresses it will discover an eternal principle of beauty which animates all these sensual forms. This eternal principle is the Divine. The Libra will learn that if a thing is of God – if it is good and true – it will be beautiful. If it is beautiful it is also good and true. This contemplation of beauty will also be a profound service to the world, for the essential beauty of the world will be more recognized. Thus the world will seem more beautiful to mortals.

The Yoga of Scorpio

Oh how easy it is to feel close to God when we are in a mansion surrounded by servants answering to our every beck and call; or, when we are in a beautiful park with the sun shining and the birds singing. Yes, when things are going well it is very easy. Natural, really. But can one feel close to God at night, when the air is filled with the death squeals of rabbits being devoured by coyotes; or in a slum on a cold winter's day when the chill numbs the very bones? Can one feel the Divine on the battlefield when best buddies are being slaughtered or disemboweled, or when a loved one is dying of cancer; or when searing pain moves through our bodies? In other words, can one feel the Divine in the depths of hell? If not, our yoga is not complete. Here in a nutshell is the yoga of Scorpio. Not pretty perhaps, but very powerful. When Jesus recognized the Divine in Lazarus (who had been dead for three days and whose body must have already been seriously decomposed), Lazarus rose from the dead, as fresh as a newborn. When he saw the Divine in the lepers (outcasts of society) they were immediately healed. When he saw the Divine in the lame person, the lame person "leaped as a hart" and bound on his way, singing God's praises. When he recognized his divine destiny on the cross, he resurrected and death lost any power over him. This ability to penetrate beneath appearances and see the Divine – which the testimony of our senses and of the whole "consensus reality" of things denies – is the special yoga of Scorpio. And they, more than most, have the power to do this. And this is their service to the world.

For the Scorpio who is on the path, negative appearances and conditions are wonderful things. They are only fuel for his or her "being awareness;" fuel for deeper realization and penetration; the lead from which he or she will create gold.

For the Scorpio who has attained, heaven and hell are equal. Whether he or she is one place or another has no bearing on his or her well-being or perception. Everything becomes heaven.

The Yoga of Sagittarius

Sagittarius, being a Fire sign, will get good results from agni yoga in all its various forms. The contemplation of light, color and the different rays of the Divine will bring the soul closer to the Divine. But Sagittarius is also a jnani yogi at heart. It loves wisdom. All the paths of wisdom – the reading of scripture and sacred writings, the study of philosophy and first principles – are all valid paths for Sagittarius. The common forms of religion and metaphysics work particularly well for the Sagittarian as it feels right at home here.

The Yoga of Capricorn

Being an Earth sign Capricorn excels at the yoga of Earth that we discussed previously. It also excels at karma yoga, for unlike the other Earth signs, it loves action.

What is commonly called "cosmic consciousness" – the

perception of the order and beauty of the universe – comes under Capricorn. Its own innate sense of order (in many cases an unconscious drive) comes from this soul perception. Its highest aspiration is to manifest this Divine Order in its own microcosm. No one can do this better than Capricorn.

For the Capricorn, time is not a prisoner but a liberator and an instrument of order. The enlightened Capricorn is very aware of the "timeless" but also understands that manifestation happens in "time" – in a regular order and sequence. All Good is always present, but manifestation is an orderly process. No one benefits more from rite and ritual than does the Capricorn. A religious rite is merely a "right order" that has been discovered and implanted into the mortal consciousness through repetition. This is its purpose.

When the ancients discovered elements of the cosmic order, they immediately created a rite-ritual to teach the common people. Today, even in the secular world we see this phenomenon. The inauguration of a president is very much like a religious ceremony. Clear thinkers discerned that there was a correct and harmonious way to transfer power – and thus a rite (though a secular one) was instituted. There is a correct way for a nurse to draw blood from a patient, a correct way to perform a surgery, a correct way to solve a mathematical problem – all of these are anchored into consciousness through ritual – repetitive actions.

If one observes properly we see that we are surrounded on every side by rite and ritual – from the way the checkout clerk operates in the supermarket, to the way we dispose of the dead. Following a right order brings us closer to the Divine Order, which brings us closer to the Divine Orderer himself. This is the path of Capricorn.

The Yoga of Aquarius

Aquarius, being an Air sign, excels in the yogas of the Air signs

– panayama, breathing exercises and jnana yoga.

Astrology itself, the contemplation of the universe and its movements – the meanings derived therefrom – is also a valid yoga for Aquarius and one in which it will excel. Astrology, rightly understood, is a form of jnana yoga. Aquarius will begin with the outer study of the planets and their movements. But as the yoga progresses, they will see into the inner side – every planet a divine principle – every sign a divine function and perspective on things. From the study of the creation, the mind will naturally begin to contemplate the Creator.

Where the path of Cancer leads to the adoration of the Divine Mother, and the path of Leo to the adoration of the Son, the path of Aquarius leads to the adoration of the Heavenly Father – the origin of all things, the Prime Cause and Mover. To be "original" means to think from and come from the "origin." This is why Aquarians tend to be so original and unique.

There is much to be written on Astrology as a yoga in itself, but we will confine ourselves to the basics. No student of Astrology can fail to see the wisdom with which the universe was created. When one contemplates the mathematics and engineering involved in such an undertaking – whether it be the macrocosm or the microcosm – one is in awe. This is not the creation of a limited human "left brain" but of something vast, mighty and powerful. A divine mind and a divine will. A vast Self-knowledge. And this mind, will and knowledge are not separate from us, but right where we are – part of us. Eventually we learn that it IS us. THAT is being us. This is the path of Aquarius.

The Yoga of Pisces

Pisces, being a Water sign, is a natural bhakti yogi. Love and devotion is a valid path and Pisces is good at it. But the yoga of Pisces will take it further than the other eleven signs. In Pisces the soul will transcend God himself. It will transcend the Father, the

Mother and the Son and go right into the "unmanifest" before such things exist. In the beginning the Pisces will think he or she is meditating on "chaos" – for in this transcendent unmanifest, there are no gods, no gender, no archangels, angels, planets, or star systems.

There is no Order and no Orderer. There are no barriers or distinctions – no form. Thus there can be no judgment, no karma, no gender differentiations, and therefore, no suffering. It is a great Zero. Nothing we can say about it. It is the Zero from which all numbers emanate. It is the emptiness which allows all things to be. It is the Zero from which God himself comes. It is the final mystery.

The Twelve Philosophies of Health

The twelve signs of the zodiac represent twelve powers of the soul; twelve perspectives and attitudes to life; twelve ways that the Divine functions; twelve philosophical positions. Of late I am also seeing them as twelve different cultures. For these twelve philosophies produce "culture" as a natural side effect. And watching the interplay of these different philosophies regarding anything in life is very much akin to watching a "culture clash" among people of different nations. Only we often see these "culture clashes" within the same community and even the same family. How can we soothe these clashes? How can we bring harmony there?

Through knowledge and understanding.

The health field, like many other areas of life, seems, to the uninitiated, like a jungle. Different therapies, supplements, vitamins, minerals, homeopathic remedies, diets and lifestyles are all touted as the cure to whatever ails you. On the surface this is a cacophony of conflicting voices and messages. But the insights of Astrology will show the harmony here.

For in health, as in every area of life, there are twelve philo-sophical positions – twelve approaches, twelve modalities. Each of these is represented by one of the signs of the zodiac.

In general the Fire signs (Aries, Leo and Sagittarius) focus more, and respond to, what we call "energy medicine." There is a natural flow of energy through the body (bodies). When this gets blocked up the person can manifest symptoms. The theory goes that if the natural flow of energy is restored, the symptoms disappear. This is workable in many cases. Therapies that do this (acupuncture, acupressure, reflexology, kinesiology to name a few) are powerful for these people. There are also therapies that "add" energy to the body (laying on hands, reiki, polarity therapy to name a few) and these are also very good here. In this philosophy, a person's energy level is the main defense to disease. A person with a strong energy level will be immune to most problems. These people also have a very strong connection to the healing power of Fire. Heat, warm climates, thermal-oriented therapies are very good for them.

The Earth signs (Taurus, Virgo and Capricorn) are focused more on the physical level of the body. The physical dimension. The "machinery" and structure of the body. They gravitate to healing modalities such as naturopathy, crystals, massage, and to the healing powers of nature in general. They have a special connection to the healing powers of the Earth itself – the mountains, the forests, the mud and the soil. They feel that if symptoms arise there is some "substance" that needs to be added or taken away or brought into balance. It's a physical approach to healing – pretty much what is prevalent in the culture today – and it has much validity.

The Air signs (Gemini, Libra and Aquarius) are much concerned with mental health and the role that the mind plays in healing. On some level, they understand that though disease ends up in the physical body, it rarely (almost never) originates in the body. There are impurities in the mind, the thinking and the speech that are at the root of most problems. They respond well to therapies that deal with these things. Good health for them is not just the absence of symptoms, but the ability to think clearly and communicate properly. Though the body may be free of symptoms, if the thinking is not clear, or the judgment not sound, there will be pain and unease. People strong in the Air signs have a special connection to the healing powers of the Air and respond well to these kinds of therapies – air baths, staying out in windy places, breathing exercises and the like. The air contains a prana that nourishes the body and disease is often the manifestation of "lack of prana." Another valid approach.

The Water signs (Cancer, Scorpio and Pisces) tend to focus on emotional health and well-being. Good health means emotional wellness. Disorders or inharmonies in the emotional life will wind up in the body as some condition. Here we see the modalities that search for "root emotional" issues – psychology, past-life therapy, etc. – behind a given disease. And there is much validity here. These people have a very strong connection to the healing powers of water. They benefit from being near the sea, rivers or lakes. Soaking in hot tubs, mineral springs, whirlpools and the like are wonderful therapies for them.

Now let us take a look at the twelve health philosophies on an individual level.

Important to understand that when we talk of an "Aries or Taurus philosophy" we don't necessarily mean a person who has the Sun in Aries or Taurus. A person can be any Sun sign and still have an Aries philosophy when it comes to health. For example, if Aries is on the Sixth House cusp or if the Ruler of the Sixth House is in Aries, these people would have Aries attitudes to health. The same is true of each of the other philosophies. Also important to understand that it is rare for any individual to be a "pure" type. Most of the time, we are a blend of different philosophies – but to see this we need to cast the individual chart and look at the specifics.

The Aries Philosophy of Health

When Aries is connected to health, good health is not about the absence of physical symptoms. Though a person may get a clean bill of health from the doctor – no cancer, no heart disease, every organ OK – if he or she is out of shape, the person is not healthy. Good health means physical fitness, the ability to run, bike or swim x amount of miles – or to bench-press x amount of pounds. It means good muscle tone, physical strength and endurance. It means athletic ability. Thus these kinds of people benefit much from vigorous physical exercise. A day at the gym can often be as beneficial for them as a visit to the health professional.

Many of these people are into diet and supplements, but these are not so much for health, but more about enhancing performance. There is something very wonderful about this concept. They demonstrate energy, vigor and physical power. But if overdone – and we see this often – it can actually create health problems later on down the road. If Mars is afflicted in the horoscope, these people can create long-term damage to the knees, hips and other organs through too much exercise. Their athletic zeal often leads to accidents. They are so intent on "excelling" and competing that they push the body beyond its normal limits. So, while they should exercise and strive for physical fitness, they need to be careful not to overdo it. As with all the other Fire signs, they benefit from heat and thermal-type therapies. Fire ceremonies, candle-burning rites, sweat lodges and saunas are all natural tonics. Hot and spicy foods also tend to be tonics for these people.

The Taurus Philosophy of Health

The Taurus philosophy of health tends to be a "material" approach. It is "substance-oriented." If there is something wrong with the body there is some pill, potion, herb, vitamin or supplement that can remedy it.

They respond very well to "hands on" kinds of healing. Massage, especially deep tissue massage – chiropractic, reflexology, Shiatsu and the like. They are not usually concerned with the esoteric origins of disease, but just want the problem "fixed." When they are involved in alternative therapies they respond well to naturopathy. They instinctively understand the healing powers of nature – the herbs, rocks, stones, forests, etc. They like their therapies to be "tangible" – vague, metaphysical kinds of therapy like prayer, speaking the word, reiki are generally not appealing to them. These are much too abstract. Taurus rules the throat. And thus if they are on a spiritual path they can have excellent results with mantra therapy. Mantra therapy is different from prayer in that the sound itself – something tangible – heals. The neck, ruled by Taurus, is very much affected by the cerebellum, the seat of the subconscious mind. This is a place where tension tends to collect and neck massage is especially healthy for them. Like all the Earth signs they benefit from mud baths, mud packs, mineral baths, crystal therapy and by being in places where the Earth energy is strong – caves, mountains, old forests and the like. Like all the Earth signs, they need to monitor the mineral content of the body more than most. The Taurus philosophy of health has great validity. Nature and the Earth itself is a great pharmacopoeia. It is very effective if the cause of the unease is in the physical or etheric bodies. It is very effective in treating symptoms. But it fails when the origins of the disease are in the higher, more subtle bodies.

The Gemini Philosophy of Health

In the Gemini philosophy of health we enter (as with all the Air signs) the domain of mental health. Though a person can swim the English Channel, climb Mount Everest, and win the Tour de France year after year, though he or she has no physical symptoms, though he or she has a pill or potion for every conceivable malady, unless the person can think and commu-nicate in a clear way – interact with others on the intellectual level – there is no health. And this is simple to understand. If people are not communicating with each other properly there will be all kinds of misunderstandings and conflicts on the intel-lectual level – and often these lead to conflicts on the physical plane. Even if the person is hale and hearty, many such conflicts are going to deplete precious energy (in the best-case scenario) or lead to physical injury in the worst case. (If the person is very strong it will lead to physical injury of others, which by the karmic law will eventually return to him.) If a person doesn't have correct information, or if he or she is not processing infor-mation correctly, many other dimensions of "unease" will occur. Let's take one or two examples to illustrate. If a person misreads his or her bank statement and believes that he has $10,000 in the checking account instead of only $1,000, he or she will make decisions that will cause pain and suffering. Most likely he or she will overdraw on the checking account resulting in bounced checks, fees, expenses, and the normal outrage from irate merchants or other recipients of these checks. While we may not consider this a "physical ailment," it is an ailment on the mental level. Sound, rational judgment is affected. There is unease in the soul. If it continues, it will lead to unease in the physical body. If a person is given a bad roadmap (even through no fault of their own) the person is going to make a wrong turn and find him or herself a "stranger in a strange land." In cold and inhospitable climates. Such mistakes can even lead to death. So good health in this philosophy is about clear thinking and good communication. With sound judgment a person will eliminate many ills and pitfalls in life. Likewise with good communication. With good information, a person will know what pill, potion or therapy to use when he or she feels under the weather.

The Gemini philosophy doesn't negate the Aries and Taurus philosophies, but adds the dimension of mind to it. In a medical emergency having the right information handy is just as important as physical fitness or having the right substance. The Gemini philosophy understands that physical problems have their origin in mental problems and seeks to apply the remedy there – on the level of the mind. Mental purity, right thinking, ideas of truth are most important here. The health of the mental body is emphasized. The mental body, like the physical body, has its needs on its level. It needs to be fed (with good mental food, not junk food), it needs exercise (right use) and it needs elimination (expression). If the mental body is not being given its due, there will be vague feelings of unease, though there is no "apparent" reason for it (there are no overt physical symptoms, the person is strong and athletic, etc.). The mental body is crying out "Feed me, take care of me."

When the Gemini philosophy of health is strong in a person, blockages in communication can have an impact on health. These kinds of people either need good friends with whom they can communicate on an intellectual level or to keep a diary and communicate that way. On a deeper level, studies such as General Semantics are vital to these kinds of people. In most cases it is impossible to attain clarity of thought and expression, because the mechanism of language itself is not understood. Language is important but it has serious limitations – and these are explored in General Semantics. This kind of study is like taking a "vacuum cleaner" to the mind – something very important here. There are therapies, such as "body talk," that would also be powerful here. One gets into a meditative state and actually opens up communication with each of the organs – as if they were people. During this interaction one can find out what the organ needs, what is causing the problem and what can be done about it. The practice of praising and thanking each of the organs (as you would a person) is also very powerful. Organic life – all organic life – responds to the word and to praise.

These kinds of people tend to be more susceptible to nerve disorders and insomnia that come from a hyperactive, over-stimulated mind. Mental activity is good, but shouldn't be overdone.

The Cancer Philosophy of Health

In the Cancer philosophy of health the soul discovers a new dimension of what health is all about. Though the person is physically fit (Aries), physically at ease (Taurus) and mentally competent (Gemini), unless there is a "feeling" of wellness, unless the moods and emotions are in harmony, there is no real health. An emotional discomfort is just as much a discomfort as something physical or mental. (Often it is even worse.) It is not only a discomfort on its own level, but will eventually manifest in the physical body as some organic disorder. So, in this philosophy, there is a focus on emotional well-being – on the root emotional causes of a physical disorder – and on general emotional health. This is the realm of psychology. It is not enough for this kind of person to have no physical or mental symptoms – there is a need to feel right and to remove emotional suffering. In this philosophy (and it is very valid) the person discovers that the root cause of a present emotional (and even physical) disorder is in the past, in childhood experiences, in relations with the parents or other family members. Since the sign of Cancer rules the stomach, there is generally a big interest in diet. And, in truth, diet is more of an issue for these people than with most people. Diet is an important part of any Cancerien health regime. In the stomach we begin the process called digestion. So what we eat is important to the stomach. (Often more important for these people is HOW they eat, but this is beyond our discussion here.) From a spiritual perspective, the stomach represents our ability to "digest" and "assimilate" experience. Experiences are a food for the soul. There is a certain "nutrition" to be derived from them – a wisdom if you will. There is an essence in them that the soul needs for its proper ongoing. If experiences are not being digested they can turn toxic. Just as is the case with physical food that is not digested. So the Cancer philosophy of health involves not only the proper digestion of physical food, but the proper digestion of soul food – the experiences of life. In earlier times, when life was more simple, people had more time to digest their soul experiences. But in this day and age when everything is so hectic and the inner life has been shoved into the background the Cancer philosophy of health has become ever more important. Many things that are diagnosed as disease are simply "undigested" experience.

The Leo Philosophy of Health

Regardless of our outer circumstances in life – whether they be high or low, rich or poor – we have come here to express joy and creativity. Those with the Leo philosophy understand that we are not victims of circumstances, but creators of them. So, for these people, it matters not whether the body, mind or emotions are pathology free – they will ask the question, "Am I having fun?" "Is there joy in my life?" If the answer is in the negative, they will not feel that they are truly healthy. In fact, too much exposure to depression can be an actual cause of physical pathology with this type. In this philosophy, we learn of something not emphasized in modern medicine, or in the general health literature – the healing power of joy. Some people are creative either because it's their job, or because it's an interesting way to kill time. But with Leo, creativity has actual therapeutic value. For creativity in and of itself is a joyous act. Blocked creativity is one of the main causes of pathology with this type (not the only cause, but a major one). If health problems arise, they should definitely look at this area (also whether they are depressed). Unblock the creativity and health immediately improves.

There is an interesting book by Norman Cousins, a famous editor and writer. He was diagnosed with colon cancer and given very little hope of recovery. On an inspiration he went to the library and loaned all the old Abbot and Costello and Three Stooges movies that he could find. He spent hours every day watching them and belly laughing. And it was the belly laughing – the sheer joy – that eventually cured him. George Burns, who lived to be 100 (and smoked like a chimney), was asked for the secret of his longevity. He replied, "You gotta enjoy what you do. It's gotta be fun."

Treating a person with the Leo philosophy with drugs, herbs, substances, massage, etc. will not do the trick, if that is the only therapy. Giving them therapies that destroy the quality of life (rigid Spartan diets, chemotherapy, medicines that taste very bad and soulless regimes) will actually make them sicker. As with all the Fire signs, give them energy medicine or acupuncture and figure out ways that they can bring joy back into their lives. Restore the joy – unblock the flow of creativity – and you will have a healing. With these kinds of people, a night out on the town or the dance studio will often be as efficacious as a visit to the health professional.

People with the Leo philosophy are often very powerful healers in their own right. Of course we need to see the position of the Sun and the aspects to it for more detail, but in general they have a healing presence. Their life force is strong – so vital – that they often heal by merely touching someone. Many doctors with this position have told me this – the patient is cured when I touch them, but I go through the motions of examination and prescribing pills, because that is what is expected.

On a purely physical level, the Leo philosophy (like Aries) benefits from heat and sunshine. If they are deprived of sunshine for too long it can cause pathology. Like the Aries they do better in warmer climates and if they are forced to live in cold climates they need to bundle up more. Sunshine, saunas and thermal therapies are all natural tonics for them.

The Virgo Philosophy of Health

This is pretty much the philosophy that is prevalent today. The Virgo philosophy is about cleanliness, hygiene, purity of diet and surroundings. Personal cleanliness – internally and externally – is 90% of the healing art. Keep your utensils clean, disinfect everything, eat pure foods and you will be pretty much immune to most things. Brush your teeth, go for regular cleanings and chances are you will never get cavities. Like the Taurus, the Virgo approach to health is basically "physical and substance" oriented. They see the cause of disease to be something physical. You caught a germ and thus you got sick. You didn't brush your teeth so bacteria collected and caused tooth decay. You didn't cleanse a wound properly and so you got an infection.

Virgo is very much on the right track here, but the tendency is to apply it only on the physical level of reality. If they took this same approach to the emotional, mental and metaphysical levels, this philosophy would be awesome indeed. They would see a great reduction in disease. The only problem is that maintaining this kind of purity, on all the levels, is a great discipline, a lifetime's work, and few undertake this at the present time.

They benefit from "hands on" types of healing – things that work directly on the physical body. Since Virgo rules the small intestine – a place where digestion is taking place – diet is a big issue for them too. Foods that are difficult to digest are not good for them.

Like Taurus and Capricorn, people with the Virgo philosophy have a strong connection with the Earth element. They benefit (more than most) from being in places where the Earth energy is very strong – old forests, mountains, caves and the like. They benefit from mud baths, mud packs, and crystal therapies and from soaking in springs heavily laden with minerals (like the Dead Sea in Israel, or our own local Warm Mineral Springs in Florida, or Baden-Baden, and such places).

The Libra Philosophy of Health

Like Leo, people with the Libra philosophy understand that health is more subtle than just physical well-being. Good health for the people of the Libra philosophy also means good social health. A healthy love life. Healthy relationships. Though they go to the doctor and get a clean bill of health, if the love and social life is not up to par, they don't feel healthy. In fact, too much of this can actually lead to physical pathologies. There is a powerful connection between love and health. This is so for every person in some degree, but for the people with the Libra philosophy it is very dramatic. If a person with the Libra philosophy is under the weather, it is pretty safe to assume that underlying this condition is some marital or social inharmony. Something is blocking them from their natural expression of love. And this needs to be cleared before any real – any deep – healing can happen.

For the Libra, life has to be beautiful. If they are forced to stay in unaesthetic surroundings for long periods of time, they can actually manifest physical symptoms. They are highly sensitive to things like color, sound, and shape. Since this can cause problems, it can also effect the cure. If a person with the Libra philosophy feels under the weather, let them go to someplace beautiful – a park, a museum, an art gallery, a concert – and spend some time there. There is nothing special that they need to do. Just absorb the vibrations of Beauty. There are many stories of Libra children who were manifesting all kinds of symptoms and no doctor could cure them. They were only cured when the walls of their rooms were repainted to another, more harmonious color.

Beauty itself is a powerful healing force. Beauty is the nature of the Divine. A separation from Beauty is, in a sense, a separation from the Divine – and this separation (as we will see later when we discuss Pisces) is the root cause of every physical problem. Libra, more than most, are very sensitive to this particular separation.

As with Leo, Libra will benefit from creativity – painting, dance, music, jewelry making. The creation of Beauty is not only fun but deeply therapeutic. There is a whole science of sound and color therapy which would be wonderful for them. Mandala meditation – where you focus your mind on beautiful and proportional mandalas – are also especially beneficial.

As with the other Air signs, mental health is important to people with the Libra philosophy. The mind needs to be sound as well as the body. Also (as with the other Air signs) they benefit from the healing powers of the Air element. Air purity is more important for them than for most people. Being in windy places, taking air baths, doing breathing exercises will be natural tonics for them if they feel under the weather.

Diet, to the Libra, is only important in so far as it affects their personal beauty. The health issues of diet take second place to that.

The Scorpio Philosophy of Health

The Scorpio philosophy of health is diametrically opposed to the Taurus philosophy. In Taurus when something is amiss, we add something to the body – a pill, an herb, a supplement. Taurus sees disease as some "deficiency" in the physical body and seeks to correct it. People with the Scorpio philosophy see disease as something in the body that doesn't belong there – bacteria, germs, effete material, stones in the colon, tumors, etc. For the Scorpio, good health merely means getting rid of these things. Get rid of – eliminate – that which doesn't belong and good health is naturally restored. It is not about "adding" things to the body. This is the philosophy of the surgeon. Most surgery (not all) is about eliminating something from the body – a tumor, plaque, clots, polyps, etc. When the impediment is removed health is restored. Surgery is, of course, the most physical method of elimination. But there are others. Detoxification regimes – whether herbal or mechanical – aim at the same result. Fasting is said to be "like a surgeon's knife." All these kinds of regimes which aim at detoxification and elimination fall under Scorpio. As with Virgo, this philosophy needs to be applied to more than just the physical level if it is to be truly effective. It needs to be applied to emotional and mental levels as well. (Many are doing this with amazing results.)

For people with the Scorpio philosophy of health, good health also means good sexual health. A healthy sex life. Too little or too much is not good. In this day and age, good sexual health has become quite a challenge. The sex chakra of the planet has become very polluted. It has become dangerous to engage in the sexual act from a merely "animalistic" perspective. The rise of sexually transmitted diseases has reached epidemic proportions.

And there are hosts of lesser known ailments that also stem from impurities in the sexual act. Prostate, cervical and urinary conditions come from this (on a metaphysical level). So ultimately people with the Scorpio philosophy will need to elevate the sexual act so that it comes from a higher (less polluted) vibration. There are many systems – Eastern and Western – that have this objective, but these are beyond our scope here. There are various mechanical methods of "safe sex," but since these will not raise the vibrations of the sexual act they are less effective.

As with the other Water signs, good emotional health is very important to Scorpio. Also they benefit (more than most) from the healing powers of water. Swimming, soaking in the tub, in natural springs or lakes, or just being around water is very therapeutic.

The Sagittarius Philosophy of Health

In the Sagittarius philosophy of health a person begins to explore some of the deeper mysteries of "wellness." In Gemini, there is a focus on healthy mental functioning – the ability to think, reason, communicate and make sound judgments. This is the role of the lower mind. In the Sagittarius philosophy of health the focus is on the health (and purity) of the "upper mind" – the part of the mind that grasps abstract principles, that is concerned with the "meaning" of the information that the Gemini mind collects. This is the mind that formulates a person's "personal religion" – a person's "personal philosophy" of life.

We don't read much in the literature about this (mostly we read about the power of this pill, herb, potion, remedy or therapy), yet it is ultra-important. Much more important than mere mental or emotional health. For in this mind we form the philosophical basis by which we will interpret the events in our lives. This will, in turn, shape our psychological responses and mental decision-making. It is the "backdrop" of all our responses, whether they be healthy or pathological.

For the Sagittarius philosophy of health it is most important to evolve a correct "philosophy" of health and disease. Does disease originate in the physical body? Is it caused by germs? Bacteria? Is it caused by material substance or does it have other causes? Invisible causes?

Is the human being merely a "naked ape" – a thinking animal, with no soul – or is he something more? Is the body merely a machine, a mechanism which we treat the same way that we treat a car? Is there more to the body than we see with the naked eye or with scientific instruments?

What role does a person's beliefs play in health and disease? What role does the mind itself play in health and disease?

These are the things that are important to the people with the Sagittarius philosophy of health. Somewhere deep in their psyche is the knowledge than they are in essence "metaphysical beings," subject only to the laws of metaphysics. Hence they understand that if disease happens there has been some violation of metaphysical law, and they set out to correct it.

If a person with the Sagittarius philosophy is under the weather, his or her first response might be to call the pastor of the church or attend a prayer meeting. Others might run to the naturopath or doctor. Indeed prayer is a very powerful tonic for these people. It is true that prayer can be answered through the naturopath, doctor or healer – but prayer is the primary cause. And there are many, many stories – too many to merely dismiss as anecdotal – where prayer alone – with no substance or therapy used – has effected a cure.

People with the Sagittarius philosophy of health need to take special care of the health of the upper mental body (in astrological parlance, the Jupiter body). First off they need to feed it properly – they need to read the inspired philosophers, theologians and prophets. They need to be able to discuss their theological ideas and insights with others (expression). They need to periodically "detox" the upper mental body of false theological concepts and beliefs.

Disorders in the upper mental body can have very dire consequences – not just on a personal health level, but also on the health and well-being of masses of people. We need look no further than to Osama bin Laden, whose behavior can be traced to just such a disorder. It is the way that he interpreted the Koran that caused the problem. Humanity has witnessed many such disorders in its history – the Inquisition and the Crusades come to mind, but there are many others.

Correcting disorders in the upper mental body requires more than just herbs, potions or pills. Even the most wonderful physical therapies will not touch this body. The person needs what we call a "philosophical breakthrough." Prayer, a sincere heart, a love for truth, persistent study and inner light are the only forces that can heal the upper mental body. Its main pathology (as with the lower mental) is error – often called "sin" by religious people. This is the true meaning of sin. There is some erroneous belief or concept that leads a person to violate natural and spiritual laws.

A person with the Sagittarius philosophy of health cannot be considered "cured" unless he or she emerges from the healing with a new outlook on life, a new perspective, a new and better philosophy. This is true of everyone in some degree, but especially for these people.

Energy medicine, thermal therapies, sunshine and fire are all excellent tonics. But they will only grant "relief" and not true cure unless the philosophical outlook is changed.

The Capricorn Philosophy of Health

Generally at this time, from a behavioral perspective, people with the Capricorn philosophy of health gravitate to traditional, orthodox medicine. They tend to be conservative when it comes to health and gravitate to those therapies and systems that have stood the test of time.

In this philosophy there is a materialistic, mechanistic approach to the body and to health in general. The body has a "structure-function-order" and if any of these are out of place, they need to be corrected. If the heart is beyond repair, replace it with a new one. Likewise with the kidneys or any other organ. The body is a machine and the doctor is the repair shop.

This philosophy works very well for certain things. If a person breaks his arm, if there is structural damage, it needs to be set and put into a cast. If someone is injured in battle or in an accident, there is structural damage that needs to be dealt with. If bacteria or viruses are invading the body, these entities need to be killed so that the body has a breather with which to heal itself. The metaphysical causes of these things are not taken too much into account – we repair the damage and we've done our job.

Here there is a great emphasis on anatomy and physiology. We need to know how the body actually works so that the problem can be corrected.

There is even a spiritual position behind all of this apparent materialism. For the person with the Capricorn philosophy holds that the eternal soul fashioned the body as a machine only for this incarnation and it has no other importance. As long as the soul needs this body, it will keep it in good repair, and then dispose of it when no longer necessary. It will get a new model at the appropriate time if need be. We need not be concerned with "soul causes of disease" – just repair the body and remove the bad symptoms.

Even when a person with the Capricorn philosophy is involved in alternative medicine (and many of them are) they tend to be traditional in their approach to it. They avoid the untried and untested. When new miracle cures come out, they won't embrace them right away, but wait and see how these things work out over time.

On a deeper level, the person with Capricorn philosophy is interested in long-term cures, rather than short-term fixes. The best long-term cure is to live in such a way as to not get sick – to live a healthy lifestyle, to practice a daily and disciplined regime. So these people, more than most, are willing to undertake disciplined (and often uncomfortable) diets and health regimes. Generally they will follow the commonly accepted definitions of what this is.

The more evolved Capricorn (and there are many out there like this) will study the anatomy and physiology of man's other bodies with the same zeal and precision as he studies the anatomy and physiology of the physical body. He or she will apply the same type of "fix" in these bodies as he or she does in the physical. This is when the Capricorn philosophy becomes awesome indeed. Their virtues are lifted to higher levels, not just confined to the material world.

The Aquarius Philosophy of Health

The Aquarius philosophy of health is, in many ways, diametrically opposite to the Capricorn philosophy. While both philosophies are scientific, the Aquarius will embrace the new and the experimental, where the Capricorn will tend to reject them. The Aquarius is very experimental in his or her approach to health.

In this philosophy there is an understanding that every person is something unique – is wired up in a certain and unique way – and thus there are no "cookie cutter" approaches to health.

The person with the Aquarius philosophy sets out on one of the grand adventures of life – to learn – through trial, error and personal experimentation – how he or she personally functions, what therapies and medicines will work specifically for them. All the rule books are thrown out (sooner or later) and no tradition is especially sacred. They learn by personal experience. (They actually incarnate for this purpose – it is an important form of self-exploration and self-knowledge.)

There is a strong virtue here. For this is the way that new

knowledge, new therapies, new medicines are discovered.

In health, Aquarius is very much the way they are in other things. There is a love for the ultra-new and the ultra-old. They, more than most, are likely to rediscover healing techniques of the very ancient world and apply them today. Also they gravitate to the latest technological advancements of modern medicine – stem cells (a person with an Aquarius philosophy regardless of religion will certainly favor this), laser surgery, MRIs, genetic engineering, gene therapy and more.

Often this love for the new and the untried, this love for experimentalism will lead them to embrace ANY new diet or supplement or therapy that comes out, merely because it is new. So they need to be careful about this and do more homework.

Experimentalism is a wonderful thing. But not every experiment works – and sometimes it can even be harmful. Thus people with the Aquarius philosophy need to engage in these things in a very "mindful" and aware way. But a few failures is the price we pay for new knowledge, and the Aquarius philosophy is willing to pay this price.

The person with the Aquarius philosophy of health believes that correct scientific knowledge will cure (eventually) any disease. And since science is leading us ever closer to the quantum and sub-quantum universes, they are getting very close to the mystical and spiritual approaches to health, which we discuss next.

The Pisces Philosophy of Health

To understand this philosophy a person needs to hang around the ashrams, monasteries or convents. Here these things are openly discussed.

In many ways the Pisces philosophy is similar to the Sagittarius philosophy. Good health comes to us from "above" as it were. Where Sagittarius sees the origin of disease as "sin" – an error in the upper mental body – Pisces sees it as a "disconnection." Life, life force, energy comes to us from "supernatural sources."

The energy that a person seems to get from the natural world – from nature – is only the "side effect" of the life that comes from the Super Natural. It is the outpicturing in matter of a spiritual process.

People with the Pisces philosophy of health believe that there is ONE and ONLY ONE physician – ONE and ONLY ONE healer. This is the Divine. There is no power in drugs, herbs, medicines, or mortal human doctors per se. When the Divine grants healing, these things are often its instruments. But if the Divine doesn't grant healing, all these things – the most powerful and celebrated healer, the most potent drug – have no power. Perhaps they will grant a person some temporary relief, but no lasting cure. Therefore if health problems arise, one should not reach for the nearest pill or potion, or run to the health professional, but seek the healing within. These people are born with this knowledge, they remember on a soul level. And, in this life, they are called to bring it forth in expression. To deepen their understanding of these things.

The Pisces philosophy of health is the philosophy of the spiritual healer, the reiki practitioner, the layer on of hands, the yogi. And these people benefit greatly from these kinds of therapies.

If someone is born with the Pisces philosophy of health, good health means much more than just the absence of physical symptoms, physical fitness, emotional health, a happy love and financial life. Good health is about good spiritual health, being in a state of connection with the Higher Power, being in a state of grace. If these things are lacking the person will not feel the "wellness" – in fact, spiritual problems or inharmonies can actually be the cause of physical symptoms with these people. And they need to be looked at if problems arise.

There are many, many stories of people who received physical healing at yogic retreats, evangelical-type meetings, in a state of personal meditation, or from merely participating in the "darshan" of a saint. In these instances – and there is numerous personal testimony (I have personally experienced this too) – there was no physical substance or therapy used. The saint or minister was merely talking and in the talk, a spiritual break-through occurred – and the person received healing. The spiritual problem that was causing the disease was removed, and so the disease just went away – there was nothing to support it. If disease was "material" in origin, these things are totally impossible. But they happen, though you don't read about it in the popular literature.

The person with the Pisces philosophy of health will come to understand that the ONE healer is not limited in its expression. It can act directly on a problem (as in the cases mentioned above) or it can act through instruments. It is all a case-by-case matter.

The person with the Pisces philosophy of health is (usually) getting his or her intuition trained in health matters. We all get our intuition trained in different ways (in the horoscope we look at Neptune and the Lord of the Twelfth House to understand this) – for them it is in health and healing. Just as intuition is called the "shortcut" to wealth, it is also the shortcut to health if we are open to it. It is being open to the intuition of the moment – the still small voice – that is important to Pisces, not this system or that system. Only the intuition of the moment is important. Therapies that never before worked for such a native can, at a certain time, work. Therapies that always worked might not work at a given instance. Only the intuition – the voice of the inner teacher – can discern these things.

Intuition is important to them not only in personal health but also in their involvement in the healing of others.

For the person with this philosophy, health problems are never what they seem to be. Often it is merely the Higher Power's way of calling them closer. When it wants their attention, it might send them a health problem. When it succeeds in getting their attention, the health problem will often fall away of its own weight – it had no other reason for existence.

So health problems for these people can be understood to be only "calls to prayer and meditation" – calls to greater unity with the Higher Power.

As with all the other Water signs, Pisces benefits from water-oriented therapies. Soaking in tubs, spas, whirlpools, mineral or natural springs, swimming, boating and just being around water are naturally therapeutic for them – and often have dramatic results. Again, as with the other Water signs, there is a great focus on emotional health and in tracing back to the root emotional cause of a given problem. Only Pisces takes this a few steps further – it traces back to the original "spiritual disconnection" that is causing the problem. Ultimately, it is this that is the cause of all disease (and even death).

The Pisces believes (in his or her heart and soul) that death was not the destiny of man. Man was created to be immortal, but his disconnection brought this malady about.

The Horoscope and the Spiritual Roots of Disease

"And ye shall serve the LORD your God, and He will bless thy bread, and thy water; and I will take sickness away from the midst of thee. None shall miscarry, nor be barren, in thy land; the number of thy days I will fulfill" (Exodus 23:25–26).

The Bible is a book of profound esoteric wisdom. It was never intended to be a history book as we understand the term. It was a law book. We might find details that are not historically accurate, or great periods of history that are skipped, glossed over, or slighted – because this was never the intention of the book. The important thing about the Bible is that it is "spiritually correct."

Like any book of esoteric wisdom, the Bible is a multidimensional work. It is read on many, many levels. (This is why students of Astrology, Tarot and Kabbalah, who are used to this kind of multilevel thinking – symbolic thinking – can derive much benefit from it. In fact, I can't think of better preparation for Bible study than these kinds of disciplines.)

Like all esoteric literature, the Bible is filled with paradox and apparent contradictions. It cannot be accessed by the intellect alone. It requires effort from the reader and higher assistance to really penetrate it – to access its deeper meanings.

Paradox in the Bible serves a few functions. At one time they used to infuriate me, but now I can see the profound wisdom in them. First off, it serves to separate the real student from the dabbler – the holy from the profane; the ripe from the unripe. The dabbler will look at the paradox and say "This is so stupid, there's nothing to this" and walk away. Precisely what the prophet intended. The real student will understand that the paradox is a concealment of a deeper truth and will work to find that deeper truth. Thus the deeper mysteries are always concealed from the profane. Also these paradoxes are like quizzes – exams in school. They sharpen the mind, and enable the student to measure his or her progress. Learning to deal with paradox is one of the great life-skills that a person can learn – for life, even on the everyday level, is also filled with paradox.

When we analyze the above-mentioned scripture, especially from a modern, scientific perspective, we are confronted with many paradoxes. The scripture says that "Ye shall serve the Lord your God...and I will take all sickness from the midst of thee." Very simple. Not complicated. Please note that it doesn't say that if you eat organic rice, or go on a macrobiotic diet, or quit smoking, only then will "I take away all sickness from the midst of thee...the number of thy days I will fulfill." Nor does it say that if you have regular mammograms and checkups then "I will take away all sickness from the midst of thee." No, the prophet is giving us a whole different premise on health and healing. From this scripture good health and long life are dependent on one thing and one thing only – "service to the Lord your God."

Note that the scripture is not denying the efficacy of these things – right diet, herbs, checkups and the hosts of powerful healing modalities that are out there. Not at all. But these – good though they are – are not the essence of good health and longevity. It is something much deeper than that.

Also note the phraseology the "Lord your God" – this is not some outside being out there in the sky, but your personal God, the God within you. The God that is incarnate within each person. He is the same everywhere, but expresses himself in a unique way through each person. It is this uniqueness that constitutes a person's service. If you try to serve "another's God" – valid though it may be for that person – this promise won't hold true.

Also note that the scripture says "I will take away ALL sickness..." Not some sickness. All sickness. The statement is flat and unequivocal.

Service to God, to the Higher Self, the Higher Nature (there are many, many names for this nature and many ways of expressing this) implies "connection." When we are not serving this God, we are in a state of disconnection. And it is this disconnection that is the root cause of all disease and premature death. This disconnection can be likened to a disconnection from life itself – from the Origin of Life, from the great power source that is constantly renewing and revivifying the world – both the macro world and the micro world (each person's individual world).

The consequences of disconnection result in "death." This means a "lessening of life." The less life, the more death and decay is dominant in the organism. This is the meaning of many biblical utterances such as "The wages of sin [error, disconnection] is death," and the punishment for certain practices (idolatry, murder, certain forms of sexual misconduct, violating Sabbaths, rest periods and hosts of other things) is death. Things that disconnect a person from the source of life bring death – a weakening of the life force. When the life force is lowered a person is now vulnerable to all kinds of things, as any professional healer will tell you.

The great medieval commentator Nachmanides (AD 1194–1270) explains this scripture to mean that "the righteous man has no need of doctors" (Perush al Hatora, Parshas Bechukosai). A startling statement on the face of it, but easily understandable based on our previous discussion. The righteous man is the "connected" man. The fully connected person (man or woman) is not subject to sickness. He or she has a natural immunity and hence has no need of doctors.

Nachmanides goes on to say that such a person needs a prophet and not a doctor. That is, if some health problem occurs, what he really needs is not a new diet, herb, or therapy, but the services of someone who can show him how the disconnection occurred – the nature of the disconnection – and how to go about getting reconnected. These things are the province of the prophet and not the doctor.

In modern times we see secular science trying to treat what are in essence "spiritual problems" from a mundane medical perspective. They medicate, suppress, and manipulate chemistry and matter, all to no avail. Often there is temporary relief (and we should be grateful for that) but no permanent cure. The origin of the problem is on another level and different methods need to be used. (There is a wonderful film that highlights this issue called *The Exorcism of Emily Rose*.)

One of the beautiful things about a horoscope is that it can give us profound insight into the spiritual roots – the disconnection – of a disease. Perhaps as Nachmanides says, it is best to go to a prophet. But in the absence of this, a good horoscope seems the next best thing.

The ten planets of the horoscope relate not only to physical organs and systems, but also to spiritual and metaphysical principles. It's as if every organ is the incarnation – the form and function – of an invisible principle. Thus we can see, at a glance, the connection between the visible and the invisible.

There are many ways to analyze a chart for these things, but a very simple way is to look at the planets that are afflicted, that are stressfully aspected. These show obstructions or blockages in the normal function of these energies (and thus these organs).

If the Sun is afflicted (stressfully aspected) in the horoscope, there tend to be genetic problems with the heart and spleen. But the spiritual root causes tend to be in a "misidentification" with who the person really is – a disconnection from the true self. This can lead to either undue arrogance, as the native tries to compensate for the disconnection, or a false, destructive kind of humility. Other root causes to investigate are the blockage of legitimate creative urges, depression, feelings of disempowerment and abuses of power in the past. Power is every person's birthright, but the abuse of it is a great curse.

If the Moon is afflicted in the horoscope, stomach and breasts tend to be vulnerable organs. But the spiritual root causes of the problem lie in the abuse or misuse of the emotional energies. Often this can be traced to traumas and experiences with the mother or in childhood. Other root causes to be explored are abuses of the nurturing process – either too much or too little. If Mercury is the afflicted planet, the lungs, small intestines, arms and shoulders (and overall nervous system) tend to be vulnerable. These can be strengthened in many mundane ways, but the spiritual root causes tend to come from the abuse of speech, the tongue and the thought process. Where Moon afflictions tend to originate in the astral body, Mercury afflictions tend to originate in the mental body. As Rumi has said, "The tongue is either a treasure without end or a disease without a remedy."

If Venus is the afflicted planet, the kidneys and hips tend to be vulnerable. But the spiritual root causes of the problem lie in the love life – in disconnections from the love energy of the cosmos. Relationship problems – the traumas behind many of these things – are often at the root of the disconnection. But very often it is the disconnection from love that creates the relationship problem. The natural love force that flows through all beings needs to be restored here.

If Mars is afflicted in the horoscope, the adrenal glands, the head, sexual organs, colon and bladder tend to be vulnerable. And the spiritual root causes can come from various areas – anger, unjustified or even justified, needs to be looked at. The other main root cause comes from abuse of the sexual energies.

If Jupiter is afflicted in the horoscope, the liver and thighs tend to be vulnerable. The spiritual root causes can come from what is often called "religious pathology" – an abuse of what is basically a benevolent force. Religious fanaticism, intolerance, or using religion in a way it was not designed for – all need to be looked at. Also, impurities in the upper mental body – false beliefs, a false interpretation of life, of the meaning of life – also need to be examined. Sometimes the spiritual root cause comes from a deficiency in the upper mental body – a lack of understanding of what life is about and what the purpose is.

If Saturn is afflicted, the spine, knees, teeth, bone structure and skeletal alignment become very vulnerable. Bones can become brittle. Vertebrae get easily misaligned. Arthritis is a common ailment with these types. But the root cause tends to come from the abuse of authority in past lives (or the present one). Undue tendencies to fear and pessimism also need to be examined. The fear of change, the desire to keep everything as it is, undue conservatism, are all part of the spiritual disconnection.

If Uranus is afflicted the ankles become vulnerable. But spiritually, the root cause comes from blockages in a person's originality and inventiveness. More likely, it comes from rebellion – a rebellion against the Divine Order of things – against what a person came here to do. And the wrong kind of rebellion. There are positive and negative ways to rebel. And these things need to be looked at.

If Neptune is afflicted, the feet become vulnerable. Spiritually the root cause can be inability to transcend material conditions – a feeling that one is "locked in" to a condition. This is a disconnection from the transcendental power within all of us. Also the abuse of spiritual or soul powers needs to be looked at – there is a correct way that these things are used and an incorrect way.

If Pluto is afflicted, the sexual organs, bladder and colon are vulnerable (as with Mars). The most common spiritual root cause of the problem is the abuse of the sexual energy – and there are many forms of such abuse. Violent tendencies (on all the levels) also need to be looked at.

The horoscope can also take us deeper into this understanding when we analyze the Lord of the Sixth House – the planet that is the "keeper" of our overall health. Whichever planet rules the Sixth House will show us what spiritual root causes are most prominent and important during this life.

Once the root cause is discerned, correction can be made. Through prayer or meditation, through what is called "repentance" – a rethinking – a lasting healing becomes possible.

Notes

1. These dates are approximate. They can vary from year to year.
2. Alfred Korzybski, *Manhood of Humanity* (1921).

Dodona Books

ASTROLOGY, NUMEROLOGY AND GENERAL DIVINATION

The priestesses and priests received the oracles of the Dodona shrine through the rustling leaves of the sacred oak tree. The oracle was an early form of divination, and divination has existed perhaps as long as humankind itself. We use divination to foresee future possibilities, to answer questions about our lives, to explain the unexplainable, for revealing hidden dynamics in ourselves and others, for personal growth and to guide us onto the right pathway through life. Dodona Books offers a broad spectrum of divination systems to suit all, including Astrology, Tarot, Runes, Ogham, Palmistry, Dream Interpretation, Scrying, Dowsing, I Ching, Numerology, Angels and Faeries, Tasseomancy and Introspection.
If you have enjoyed this book, why not tell other readers by posting a review on your preferred book site. Recent bestsellers from Dodona Books are:

Palmistry: From Apprentice to Pro in 24 Hours
The Easiest Palmistry Course Ever Written
Johnny Fincham
Now anyone who wishes to can learn the secrets of Palmistry in this no-nonsense guide.
Paperback: 978-1-84694-047-7 ebook: 978-1-84694-644-8

Numerology Made Easy
Hilary H. Carter

2012. 666. Sometimes a number speaks a thousand words. This user-friendly guide to numerology teaches you to decode the language of numbers.

Paperback: 978-1-84694-717-9 ebook: 978-1-84694-718-6

Let the Numbers Guide You
The Spiritual Science of Numerology
Shiv Charan Singh

One of the oldest arts of Divination, Numerology can be found at the core of many religions. This book helps to rediscover the spiritual importance of using numbers.

Paperback: 978-1-90381-664-6

How to Survive a Pisces
Mary English

From the successful series on the signs of the Zodiac, *How to Survive a Pisces* helps you avoid common mishaps associated with relationships with a Pisces.

Paperback: 978-1-84694-252-5 ebook: 978-1-84694-658-5

The Syzygy Oracle
Transformational Tarot and The Tree of Life, Ego, Essence and the Evolution of Consciousness
Heather Mendel

In image and word, this primer on Kabbalah, Tarot and conscious evolution offers daily spiritual practices for developing trust in our intuitive wisdom.

Paperback: 978-1-78279-160-7 ebook: 978-1-78279-159-1